PIT STOP

STEVE BULLOCK

Scripture Union

Steve would like to thank the following people, for their love, prayers, help and support, without whom this book would not have been possible: Linda, Mum and Dad, Fran Wilbraham, Mark Hamill, The Christians in School Trust, The Stockport School Christian Group Leaders, St Chad's Romiley Pathfinder Group and The Easter Eggsperience Team.

Scripture Union, 207–209 Queensway, Bletchley, MK2 2EB, England.

© Steve Bullock

First published 1998. Reprinted 2001

ISBN 1 85999 2145

All rights reserved. No part of this publication may be reproduced, stored in a retrieval system, or transmitted, in any form or by any means, electronic, mechanical, photocopying, recording or otherwise, without the prior permission of Scripture Union.

The right of Steve Bullock to be identified as authors of this work has been asserted by him in accordance with the Copyright, Designs and Patents Act 1988.

British Library Cataloguing-in-Publication Data.
A catalogue record for this book is available from the British Library.

Cover design by Wild Associates

Text design by Blue Pig Design Co.

Printed and bound in Great Britain by Ebenezer Baylis & Son Limited, The Trinity Press, Worcester and London.

CONTENTS

Team briefing	4
So how do I use this book?	5
Tips on running Pit Stop sessions	6
Peer pressure	9
Bullying	15
Self-worth	19
Success or failure	23
Searching for riches	27
Families	33
Friends	37
Sex	41
Loneliness and rejection	45
Jealousy	49
Lying	53
Anger	57
Death and the afterlife	61
Suffering	65
Evil and the occult	71
Temptation	76
Bad habits	81
Forgiveness	85
Prejudice	89
Jesus for me?	93

TEAM BRIEFING

Every racing car needs to be refuelled, serviced and maintained by the pits for effective performance on the race track. While they may not guarantee success, resourcing the car in such a way provides the best possible chance of being successful. In a similar way Pit Stop seeks to equip and resource the leader of a 11–13 year old group with quality components for exciting and exhilarating sessions ahead.

It seeks to do this by...

A Assuming that group members have very little Christian knowledge and experience.

The ideas expressed can be easily adapted to suit any group, whether it be a church youth group, a lunchtime meeting in school or even a residential event.

B Focusing on issues that 11–13s are starting to grapple with as they learn to cope with their changing bodies, unpredictable emotions and developing attitudes towards themselves and others.

These issues then provide a wonderful means to introduce the group members to the character of God and what he has to say about the topic.

C Using exciting, fun activities, not to trivialise such issues but to involve the young people's natural energy and responsiveness in a corporate learning experience.

D Often providing more than one alternative activity for certain sections of a session.

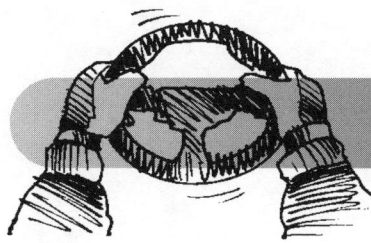

So How Do I Use This Book?

Each session will perhaps have more activities and ideas than you will have time for. This has been designed so that you can:

A Pick the activities which are most suitable for your 11–13s group.

B Be flexible depending on time.

C Extend the material of each session over a couple of weeks.

Each session may include a mixture of the following subsections/icons:

❶ Qualifying
Introductory notes for the leader.

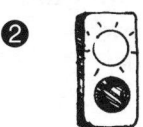

❷ Starting Grid
Ideas to introduce the topic.

❸ Lap Boards
Icons which give the train of thought behind each section, together with the total time that section will require.

❹ The Commentator
Makes important points about each section and helps the whole session run smoothly.

❺ The Chequered Flag
Summary and final challenge.

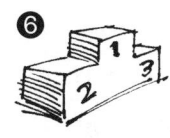

❻ On the Podium
Advises and reminds the leader as to the most appropriate place for prizes to be awarded.

❼ Lap of Honour
A worship idea if worship is appropriate for your group.
(See page 8.)

Other icons:

❽ Stop Watch
A time guide for each individual activity.

❾ Action Replay
Highlighting activity ideas which could be adapted to suit any another topic.

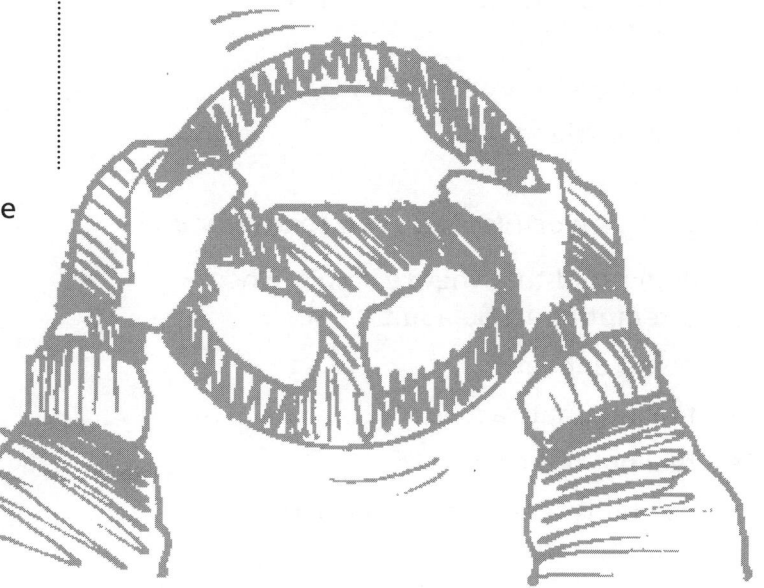

Tips on running Pit Stop sessions

Any quality work with young people needs not only to be based on prayer but also on your relationship with them. So when preparing each session, think about individual members of your group and consider the following:

A Their physical development

Group members will be experiencing rapid bodily and intellectual growth. They will develop the ability to understand abstract concepts and start asking hard questions. They will develop an increasing need to find their identity and place in the world at the same time as they experience fluctuating, unpredictable emotions. Throughout all this change they need to know they are valued, important and appreciated.

A sense of value can be created by:

- being treated as an adult.
- being listened to.
- being complemented for their appearance.
- belonging and being accepted.
- being able to do what they're good at.
- being able to meet reasonable expectations.
- being given responsibility.
- having friends.

A sense of worthlessness can come from:

- being told that they're stupid when attempting to be adult.
- being unheard.
- feeling unattractive.
- feeling 'out of it'.
- having to live up to other people's expectations.
- being reminded of a bad past record.
- not being trusted.
- being lonely.

B Their spiritual development

Obviously each session needs to take into account where the group members are spiritually so that your approach and content can be adapted to suit.

While presenting a Christian viewpoint on each topic is a key aim of *Pit Stop*, equally important is your personal witness to your group members, which if you are living a faithful obedient life in Christ, will show (Matthew 5:14–16). Therefore both the fun and serious elements of *Pit Stop* are equally important as the Holy Sprit can use you in both, to communicate the reality of the risen Christ. I hope this fact will free you from guilt if you find that group members respond better to the lively activities than to the biblical explanations.

C Their home background and acquaintances

This sensitive information will come through your developing relationship with the group members, but is very useful as it will aid your understanding of the group and will allow you to tackle issues in an appropriate and gentle manner.

Tips on running Pit Stop sessions

D Their interests

By finding out what interests your group in the realms of music, fashion, sport, hobbies, TV, films, computers etc you will be able to relate what you want to communicate in a way appropriate and relevant to them.

TIP Often if you plead ignorance and ask group members about a specific subject, they will take great delight in informing you of the facts. This can help you in your own research but will also help form relationships between you and your group members.

RUNNING THE ACTIVITIES

Some of the activities found in *Pit Stop* may seem quite daunting at first, but remember, it's harder to explain an activity than it is to practically run. Here are a few suggestions to keep in mind when attempting some of the activities:

A Understand the workings of the activity and the point which it is trying to make.

Practise the activity beforehand.

B Explain the basic concept of the activity.

C Explain the basic rules and point scoring.
D *In practice, it's better to keep the explanation of the concept and the rules to a minimum because players can get confused. Often understanding of the activity comes as soon as the activity is underway. If there are any further rules, these can be explained.*

E Split the group into teams of equal abilities.

F Run the activity and don't let it drag. *The most successful games occur when everyone is involved and enjoying themselves. To ensure that this happens, the leader often has to take control of the game and actively keep things moving along.*

TIP As a leader, continually explain what is happening, telling people what to do and if necessary hurry decisions being made by the teams.

G Be flexible with time and your session plan.

H Award any prizes at the end of the session or after you've explained the point of the activity, as the prospect of prizes and the potential loss of them will maintain a level of order.

Tips on running Pit Stop sessions

MATERIALS USED

Please be forward-thinking when you use this resource, as some activities will require you to obtain certain materials beforehand. It would be a real shame if you couldn't do an activity because you couldn't get hold of sufficient quantities of materials the preceding week.

THE PLACE OF WORSHIP IN PIT STOP

Worship is important but depending on the group and the situation, eg school, it may not be appropriate. If it is appropriate then one thing is for sure, it needs to be a positive experience, encouraging the group members to make a voluntary response to God. As such singing may not be the best option for the increasingly self-conscious 11 to 13-year-olds. Instead try other creative methods as described by the 'Lap of Honour' icon.

RESOURCE FOCUS

For a comprehensive introduction to the practicalities of running a group for 11 to 14-year-olds obtain a copy of *The Art of 11–14s* by SU and CPAS.

For further ice-breaking ideas also obtain a copy of *Theme Games* by Lesley Pinchbeck, published by SU.

That's the team briefing over, put your seat belts on and get ready for the ride of your life!!

Peer Pressure

Qualifying

Peer pressure can have a very powerful influence over a young person's behaviour. In this session young people are encouraged to discover how they are affected by such pressure and whether they feel the need to conform to those around them. We encourage young people to find the love, acceptance and identity which God offers to them.

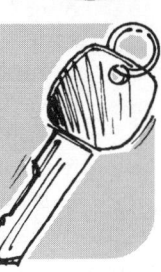

Starting Grid
(12 minutes minimum)

Ⓐ Gauntlet
10 minutes

Create a long narrow walkway, just wide enough for three members to walk side by side holding hands/wrists. Split the group into teams. Ask for four volunteers – one from team A and three from Team B. The three members from Team B stand at one end of the walkway and the volunteer from Team A stands at the other.

The object of the game is to try to reach the opposite end of the walkway first. There will be a certain amount of struggling as they meet in the middle. Team B try to move the player from Team A along with them while she tries to continue to the opposite end. For safety no one is allowed to run and Team B must hold wrists/hands and stand in a parallel line throughout.

Change players until all who want a go have played.

Ⓑ Calling the shots
Up to 10 minutes

i) Have a goalkeeper try to save as many penalties (taken by multiple penalty players from multiple penalty spots) as possible within one minute.

ii) Produce a large target and ask someone to stand in front of it. The rest of the group make paper balls and on your command throw them at the target for one minute to see how many points are scored. The target defender has to try and stop people scoring.

Commentator
2 minutes

"Today we're exploring peer pressure – the pressure exerted on someone to follow the consensus of a group of people – which can often be hard to resist."

Peer pressure questionnaire
15 minutes

Photocopy the questionnaire on page 12, give one copy to each group member and ask them to complete it. Go through the sheet with the group members and discover which of the items/behaviours they feel most and least pressurised to conform to.

Commentator
1 minute

"We all experience pressure to follow the consensus of the crowd time and again throughout our lives. Is peer pressure a good or bad thing?"

The answer to this question is that it can be both. Use the following activities to explore this further.

Thought:
Is peer pressure good or bad?

LAP 1

Total Time: 23 minutes

Peer pressure as a positive quality
10 minutes

Split the group into teams of four maximum. Place each team in a straight line and tie their hands together. Blindfold up to two of the team members and ask each team to sit down. Explain that only those with the blindfolds can talk during the activity. Give each team a task to perform, with instructions on how to build the given task. The task could be, for example, to build a tower/model using paper or *Lego* or to make a craft item.

Give them about 5–10 minutes to complete the task.

As they will discover, those who can see the instructions won't be able to tell those who are blind what to do and so all the team will have to work together in order to achieve the given task.

Commentator

2 minutes

"Peer pressure is healthy when friends help to motivate you to complete a given task. For example, those who go to slimmers' clubs find that the support they have from others who also want to lose weight, is a real incentive to achieve their ideal weight. Can you think of any other examples?"

Peer pressure as a negative quality

10 minutes

Choose three members to go out of the room with a leader. While they are out explain to the remainder that you are going to have a true/false quiz, the aim being to see if they can force the three volunteers to choose the wrong answers.

Explain that when a question is asked, you will ask people to stand on either side of the room, depending whether they feel the answer is right or wrong. Work out a secret signal so that, whichever side the volunteers choose to go to, everyone else is then to discreetly to do the opposite and encourage them to follow suit. (Use the signal after every other question.) Play until everyone realises what is happening. You will need to make up about 15 true/false questions.

Commentator

1 minute

"Peer pressure can often stop us from developing and thinking things through for ourselves. Pressure from others can force us to adapt our values and behaviour to comply with those around us, which can ultimately result in us getting involved with things we may feel uncomfortable with. Why do people choose to follow the consensus of their friends and peers?

When it boils down to it, we all want to be loved, cared for and accepted. Following the consensus of friends and peers is an expression of that because no one wants to be left out and seen as odd. But does that mean that we have to follow the crowd/consensus of opinion all the time?"

Thought:
Daniel and friends chose to obey God rather than the consensus of popular opinion

Total Time: up to 27 minutes

Turnabout

25 minutes

When playing the following game remember to a) keep this game moving quickly and b) recap the story before you ask the next question. Begin by reading together Daniel 1:1–5; 3.

Create the following on a white/black board. Fill the circles using the appropriate colours.

O	O	O	O	
BK	BU	R	BK	KEY
O	O	O	O	BK = BLACK
R	C	C	BK	BU = BLUE
O	O	O	O	R = RED
BU	C	C	BU	C = CLEAR
O	O	O	O	
BU	BK	R	R	

Split the group into three main teams. Position the teams facing you in 3 columns and designate each team a colour (black, blue or red).

The idea of the game is for the teams to answer the questions given on page 14 correctly and then try and make lines of three or four circles of their colour, in the grid, horizontally, vertically or diagonally. Each line of 3 is worth 5 points, each line of 4 is worth 10 points.

Start with the red team and ask them a question. If they get it right, they can turn one of the clear circles into a red circle. Move on to the blue and black teams respectively.

Once all the clear circles have been filled, when a team answers a question correctly they can start turning over one of the opposing teams' circles in order to try and gain points. The circles can be turned over in the following order: red to blue, blue to black and black to red.

If a team answers a question incorrectly, the same question is passed to the team on their left and so on until the correct answer is given.

Halfway through the game change the colour sequence to blue to red, black to blue and red to black.

Count up the points at the end and make a note of the winning team.

Commentator
2 minutes

"Daniel, Shadrach, Meshach and Abednego all could have saved themselves a lot of hassle by following the crowd. However they chose not to conform because they wanted to please God more than anyone else."

Thought:
God offers a love and acceptance that cannot be compared with.

Total Time: 25 minutes

The Lost Son drama (Luke 15:11–31)
20 minutes

Photocopy the drama script of this parable on page 13 and give a copy to each group member. Split the group into teams and ask them to practise/develop the drama how they want.

Allow the teams to present their master pieces to one another, and discuss the meaning of the parable.

Commentator
5 minutes

"Just like the father in the parable, God longs that everyone of us will turn to him and discover an unconditional love, acceptance and identity as members of his family.

Which option will you choose?

A The conditional option
In order to be loved, accepted and valuable you must:
- Behave in a certain way;
- Have a certain look;
- Have certain possessions;
- Fit in with those around you.

B The unconditional option
For unconditional love, acceptance and value you must:
- Just be yourself;
- Receive all these things from God by becoming part of his family."

Chequered Flag *8 minutes*

So, peer pressure is the pressure exerted on someone to follow the consensus of a group of people. This can sometimes be positive, but it can also have negative results, as it can lead people to behave in ways they usually would not.

However, the Bible has many instances of people showing great courage and strength, choosing not to be influenced by their peers as they wanted to please God first, before anyone else. The Bible explains that one reason for such behaviour is the fact that people have found and experienced God's unconditional love and acceptance which is equal to none!

Finish by putting the following words of Romans 12:2 on cards, and make enough sets for one per team. Split the group into teams and discover which team can complete the Bible verse the quickest.

Do not / conform yourselves / to the / standards of / the world / but let / God transform / you inwardly / by a / complete change / of your / mind.

On the Podium *5 minutes*

Award prizes for the following events: *Calling the shots*, *Turnabout* and the *Chequered Flag Bible verse quiz*.

Lap of Honour *15 minutes*

Read Psalm 1 to the group. Explain that it compares two sorts of people: those who choose to follow God first and those who choose not to. The psalm uses images to show the reader what both sorts of people are like.

Ask the group to think of other images which could be used to describe those who choose to and choose not to follow God. Ask them to make a picture to illustrate such an image using pencils, paints, collage materials etc.

Once they have finished their piece, ask them to explain their work to the other group members and close the time by thanking God for all the good things that are promised to those who choose to follow him.

Peer Pressure Questionnaire

ACTIVITY SHEET 1a

Complete the following questionnaire by writing down what you and your friends feel to be 'In' alongside the items listed in the left-hand column. Under the 'Pressure Rating' mark out of 10 how pressurised you feel to conform to these trends/behaviours (0 = No pressure, 10 = I have to have/do).

WHAT IS 'IN' FOR THE FOLLOWING ITEMS?	PRESSURE RATING
1 Clothes	
2 Make of trainers	
3 Music/Pop group(s)	
4 Hair style	
5 Hobbies	
6 Magazines	
7 Freetime meeting places	
8 Films	
9 Type of drink	
10 Effort given to school work	

THE LOST SON By Mark Hamill

CHARACTERS: Two narrators, Ben, Female Company (FC), Billie and Chorus

Narrator 1: This is the story of a dad and two children: Farmer Bob, Billie and Ben.

Narrator 2: Now Billie was good.
(Billie polishes her nails)

Narrator 1: But Ben was bad.

Ben: I'm bad.

Chorus: He's bad.

Narrator 2: So one day, Ben went to his dad

Narrator 2: And said

Ben: I can't wait till you're dead, so give my money now instead.

Narrator 1: Bob counted out the cash.

Narrator 2: Billie made a sigh.

Narrator 1: Ben said

Ben: Must dash.

Narrator 2: Bob waved him goodbye.

Narrator 2: Benny went to the States

Narrator 1: Where with lots of new mates

Narrator 2: He spent all his money

Chorus: On DRUGS... DRINK... GAMBLING

Narrator 1: And female company.

FC: Hi, Benny.

Narrator 2: Until the feckless Benny
Did not have a single penny.

FC: Bye, Benny.

Narrator 1: So Benny got a job

Narrator 2: Working in a sty.

Narrator 1: He thought about his dad Bob

Narrator 2: He began to cry.

Chorus: He's sad.

Ben: I'll go back home and say I'm sorry
For causing all this grief and worry.

Narrator 1: From some way off, Bob saw his son.

Narrator 2: He ran to him.

Narrator 1: Hugged him.

Narrator 2: Kissed him. And said

Bob: Let's party, everyone!

Narrator 1: Everyone was glad.

Chorus: They're glad.

Narrator 2: Except for Billie.

Narrator 1: She was mad.

Chorus: She's mad.

Billie: 'Snot fair.
How come
He's had his share?
When do I get some?

Bob: Everything I have is now yours
The land, the house, the animals
My stocks and my shares.
So cheer up Billie, don't be sad.
Now both my children, come to Dad.
(Bob puts arms around both children.)

Chorus: He's Dad.

Turnabout
(Questions taken from Daniel 1:1–5; 3)

1 The story starts with a king from a place called Babylon, which surrounds a very famous city now in Israel called…
Bethlehem
Cairo
Jerusalem?

2 This king was called…
David
Nebuchadnezzar
Jehoiakim?

3 Which country is Babylon now in…
Israel
Egypt
Iran?

So King Nebby surrounded Jerusalem, conquered and ransacked it.

4 He therefore captured the king of Judah at that time who was called…
Jehoiakim
Cecil
Abdul?

5 King Nebby then asked his chief officer to bring what into the palace for training:
elephants
Israelite men
dogs?

6 These men were to be handsome, well-educated, capable of learning and understanding. They were to be taught the language and the writings of…
The Egyptians
The Babylonians
The Italians?

7 Why were they to be trained in this way:
To fight in Nebby's army
So they could get a job in a bank
So they could serve the king?

8 How many years would the training last:
1   2   **3**?

9 Among these men were four particular people called Hananiah, Mishael, Azariah and…
Goliath
Daniel
Abraham?

Then just to complicate things they were given new Babylonian names:
Daniel = Belteshazzar
Hananiah = Shadrack
Mishael = Meshach
Azariah = Abednego

10 Some time later the king made a great statue 3m wide and how many meters tall:
18   **27**   34?

11 What was this statue made of:
silver
gold
bronze?

12 He then decided to have a special service for this statue and so he especially invited…
all his leaders/advisors
other surrounding countries
all the women of Babylon?

13 With all these people present the king announced that everyone was to bow down and worship this big statue, when…
it thundered
musical instruments were played
they thought a nasty thought?

14 Which musical instrument was not invented then:
oboe
harp
piano?

15 If anyone didn't worship, what would happen to them:
beheaded
thrown into some lions
thrown into a blazing furnace?

16 Who do you think disobeyed the order:
Shadrach
Meshach
Abednego?
(Daniel wasn't there for some reason)

17 Why didn't they obey:
They didn't know how too
They didn't hear the order
As Jews they only served the one true living God, not manmade images?

18 When the king was told of them refusing to worship this idol he ordered the furnace to be heated how many times hotter than usual:
3   **7**   9?

19 The king then ordered that all three men be tied up and thrown into the furnace by some of the king's strongest soldiers. What happened to the soldiers:
they were killed by the flames
they were killed by the king
they were killed by the three Israelites?

20 Everyone then saw how many people walking about in the furnace:
1   2   3   **4**?

21 Who was this extra person:
God
Jesus
an angel?

22 The king ordered them out of the furnace by calling them servants of:
the statue
the Most High God
Daniel?

23 Which of the following is not correct when they were examined:
Their bodies hadn't been burnt
Their hair hadn't been burnt
Their robes hadn't been burnt
They smelt of smoke?

24 As a result of this amazing miracle, what did the king basically say:
'Everyone now worship the statue'
'No other god can save his people like this'
'Blow me down, that was a bit of luck wasn't it'?

25 In fact, the king was so impressed by God that he prescribed what punishment for anyone who spoke disrespectfully of God:
Be torn limb from limb and their house be destroyed
Be thrown into the furnace
Be subjected to a slow and excruciating death?

Bullying

Qualifying

Bullying is an issue which affects the lives of many young people. This session seeks to encourage group members to face up to their experiences of bullying and guides them towards trusting in God who not only can give them strength to deal with the situation, but can also change the situation for the better. It also seeks to speak to those who bully and shows that they can change.

As this can often be a sensitive issue, be available to talk afterwards. Helpful leaflets can be obtained from Childline on 0171–239–1000, (helpline 0800 1111).

Starting Grid

(up to 20 minutes)

If you plan to play these games, don't tell them what they have in common until you are ready to move on to the next section.

Ⓐ Weak feeling games — 10 minutes

Give the young people an experience of what the bullied can feel like by playing any team game but altering the fairness of it. For example, place more members on one team than another or give one team more or better equipment required etc.

Ⓑ As big as? — 10 minutes

Split the group into teams and find out which one can:

i) make the tallest human tower or human statue (provide newspaper, tape, broom handles, old clothes etc.);

ii) crouch as low as possible in the smallest space.

Ⓒ Help! — 10 minutes

This game is very similar to a game known as Bosses and Secretaries. Give a newspaper article to person A, and a pen and paper to person B. Place both players a considerable distance apart. Surround player A with other group members, standing in a circle. Player A is then to read her article as loud as possible and player B is to try and write it down. However as soon as player A speaks, the crowd around her is to make as much noise as possible so that player B has a hard job hearing what she says.

Allow other group members to participate.

If you have a large group, it will be possible to make the noise level worse by having several of these groups playing at the same time.

Commentator — 1 minute

"Bullying is any behaviour which threatens another individual and is something that many young people experience at school. Victims of bullying may display feelings reflected in some of these first games."

Thought:
Understanding the feelings of those involved in bullying

LAP 1

Total Time: up to 16 minutes

Quantum Leap — 15 minutes

Create a situation needing six characters: a person being bullied, a friend, a gang leader, two more gang members and an onlooker. Write the characters onto six separate slips of paper and place them in a container.

Get six group members to each draw a character out of the container. Once all your characters are in position, ask them to start the role play.

At suitable points call halt. The actors stay in their positions while two more group members pick out slips of paper at random and change places with the appropriate characters. Continue to do this until everyone has been involved in the role play once or even twice.

By using this role play the young people will start to understand what the various characters may feel. For each of the characters compile a list of the feelings they experienced, and the reasons why they experienced them in the situation. This list could then be a useful starter to a discussion about the hurt bullying causes, why people do it and whether or not adults take it seriously.

Commentator

1 minute

" Bullying is not a pleasant matter and often leaves the victim hurt and often too scared to do anything about it. Does the Bible give us any hope in this situation? Or does God not care either? "

Thought:
Does God know what it's like to be bullied?

Total Time: 18 minutes

Jesus' suffering

15 minutes

Make two sets of the game cards by photocopying page 18. Make an enlarged copy of the game board as shown below. Split the group members into at least three teams.

1	EXTRA CARD 2	BULLY 3
INSULTS 8		VIOLENCE 4
7	EXPERIENCE 6	EXCHANGE 5

To play the game let each team take it in turns to roll the dice and move a counter around the game board. The aim of the game is for each team to obtain the most points in the given time. Each card is worth ten points. If a team manages to get a complete set of one type of cards, they receive an extra twenty points.

If the counter lands on a blank square, move straight on to the next team's turn.

Landing on a VIOLENCE, EXPERIENCE or INSULTS square earns the team a randomly selected card from the appropriate set.

Landing on the EXTRA CARD square earns a randomly selected card from the duplicate set.

A team landing on the EXCHANGE square can choose one other team and exchange one card with them. A team landing on the BULLY square can choose one other team and challenge them to a dice battle. Each team rolls the dice three times. The team with the highest cumulative score can take the card of their choice from their opponents.

If the teams have amongst themselves all the cards from a set and then land on that set square, then nothing happens and the next team rolls the dice. Eventually the teams will all be clamouring to land upon the EXTRA, BULLY and EXCHANGE squares.

Commentator

3 minutes

" As we have just seen, Jesus went through a horrendous time during his trial and crucifixion, suffering injustice, violence, insults and loneliness. We can safely say that Jesus knows what it is like to be bullied.

And how does God feel about bullying? Throughout the Bible we read how angry God gets when people abuse the power they have, to inflict hurt, pain and injustice upon the weak. God hates such activities and often sees himself on the side of the oppressed (Isaiah 58,59; Amos 5). "

Thought:
We can work things out with God's help

Total Time: up to 37 minutes

Shelter building

20 minutes

This activity can either be done on a large scale or on a small scale, but either way it involves the group members building shelters.

Obtain many cardboard boxes, sheets and parcel tape. Split the groups into teams and give them a selection of the materials each. Explain that you would like them to build a strong shelter, somewhere they feel that they could go to for safety whenever they felt threatened. Alternatively make small scale models out of newspaper. Give them 10 minutes to construct this.

Explain that you wish to test the strength of their shelters, therefore in turn ask one member only or all of a set of team members to go into their shelter. Provide the other teams with soft balls, tennis balls, basket balls, footballs etc. Ask them to stand away from the shelter at a set distance and on your whistle ask them to throw their projectiles at the shelter. Award points for the strongest shelters.

Beware of fire and take necessary precautions!

Quieten the group down and read Psalm 46:1–3.

Commentator
2 minutes

" God is our shelter. We can run to him anytime, as he is much stronger and bigger than our problems.

Let's find out what the apostle Paul learnt through all his trials and persecutions. "

Strong towers
10 minutes

Give each member 10 small stones or pieces of *Lego* etc. and ask them to write upon them in permanent marker pen the following words which make up the verse Philippians 4:13 NIV: 'I can do everything through him who gives me strength'.

Ask them to bond them together into a strong structure using paste, *Polyfilla* or something similar.

Commentator
5 minutes

" God can and will give us the strength to cope with the situation.

Some victims of bullying may wish they had the strength to lash out, and defeat their bullies. Strength is needed for us to ignore the mocking and insults, and to tell others such as parents and teachers about a bullying situation. It is also needed to face the questions and repercussions afterwards. Remember God wants to help, so give the situation to him and see what a difference it could make. "

Chequered Flag
10 minutes

Bullying does affect many young people, in many different ways. However if you are a victim of bullying, you can be encouraged by what we read in the Bible.

Firstly, we discover that God hates injustice and the abuse of power. He is therefore often seen on the side of the weak, helping and defending them.

Secondly, he allowed his Son to experience suffering at the hands of men similar to that which we may have experienced. We can find in him a friend who knows exactly what we may go through and therefore will know exactly the help and support that we need.

Thirdly, we discover that God can give us the strength and help that we need to help us through the situation we may find ourselves in.

Finally, we discover that God is in the business of changing bad situations and bullies for the better.

Secret envelopes

As a closing activity, give each member a pen, a piece of paper and an envelope. Ask them to write a letter to God about a) a bullying situation which is concerning them, how they feel and what they would like God to do about it; or b) how they may be sorry for bullying others. Stress that these will be confidential.

Once everyone has written something, ask them to seal their letters in their envelopes, walk out to the front and tear the letters up into small pieces into a black plastic bag, as a symbolic gesture of handing the situations over to God, knowing that he has heard them and wants to help.

On the Podium *5 minutes*

Award prizes for the following activities: *As big as?*, *Jesus' suffering* and *Shelter building*.

Lap of Honour *10 minutes*

Focus on and thank God for his strength and help by:

Photo meditation

Take enough pictures of strong objects (eg buildings, cliffs etc) for the group to have one each and lay them in the middle of the group. Ask them to pick a picture which most appeals to them, then either read Psalm 91 or play some appropriate music, during which they are to listen to the words and focus on God being our strong helper.

A helpful piece of music is: 'Let Them Come to Me' from the album called *Wonderful World* by Chris Eaton.

JESUS' SUFFERING

Jesus' experiences	Violence towards Jesus	Jesus' insults
1 Jesus was betrayed (MATTHEW 26:47–56)	1 Jesus was spat in the face (MATTHEW 26:67)	1 Jesus was mocked by the council of religious leaders (MATTHEW 26:67)
2 Jesus had enemies trying to find false evidence against him (MATTHEW 26:59)	2 Jesus was slapped (MATTHEW 26:67)	2 Jesus was stripped and humiliated (MATTHEW 27:28)
3 Jesus had lies told against him (MATTHEW 26:60)	3 Jesus was beaten (MATTHEW 26:67)	3 Jesus was mocked by soldiers (MATTHEW 27:29)
4 Jesus was disowned (MATTHEW 26:69–75)	4 Jesus was whipped (MATTHEW 27:26)	4 Jesus was insulted by the general public (MATTHEW 27:39)
5 Jesus had a crowd incited against him (MATTHEW 27:20)	5 Jesus was forced to wear a crown made from thorny branches (MATTHEW 27:29)	5 Jesus was insulted by the religious leaders (MATTHEW 27:4)
6 Jesus was surrounded by soldiers (MATTHEW 27:27)	6 Jesus was hit over the head with a stick (MATTHEW 27:30)	6 Jesus was insulted by the crucified robbers (MATTHEW 27:44)
7 Jesus felt alone and abandoned (MATTHEW 27:46)	7 Jesus was crucified (MATTHEW 27:35)	

Self-worth

Qualifying

Young people especially need to know that we are loved, cared for and valued. They are beginning to form an opinion of themselves by assessing how others treat them. This session seeks to shift their focus of attention from the potentially negative opinions of those around them to the positive opinions that God holds about us which, when grasped, can have a life-changing effect.

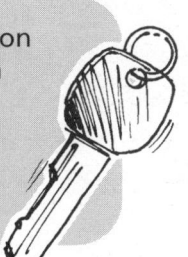

Starting Grid
(20 minutes minimum)

Every item we come into contact with is worth something to a greater or lesser degree. In the same way, we all place a value on ourselves which is called 'self-worth'.

A Valuable or not?
10 minutes

Buy an antiques magazine from a newsagent, cut out photos of antiques, mount them on card and keep a note of their price. Show these pictures to the group and ask them to place them in order of value and to guess the approximate cost of each.

B Chocolate pontoon
10 minutes

Buy up to 10 bars of chocolate, remove all the prices and display the bars to the group. Tell the group the total price of the chocolate collection and explain that the game they are about to play is similar to the card game 'pontoon'.

Each team in turn chooses a number of chocolate bars, however many they think will equal 75% of the overall total. Once they have made their choice, add up each team's figures. If they have gone over the 75% mark they have bust and lost. See which team gets the closest to the correct answer without going over it. Give all the chocolate bars to this team.

Thought:
We can think very negatively about ourselves, often because we take to heart how others react to us.

Total Time: up to 28 minutes

Advertise yourself
10 minutes

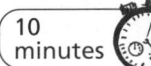

Give the group members access to old shopping catalogues, general magazines, paper, scissors, paste and pencils. Ask them to design a poster advertising themselves, using the above materials, complete with a slogan summing up their personality. Once these have been created, ask them to show their creations and, if necessary, explain them.

Commentator
1 minute

" This session is all about how we view ourselves. Sometimes we can view ourselves in a positive light, other times we can view ourselves very negatively and not feel we are that valuable at all. "

Countdown
15 minutes

Cut out pictures of famous people. Prepare a set of 26 cards, and write on each a different letter of the alphabet. Prepare another set of cards (about 10 in all) and write on each either a plus or minus symbol.

Pick volunteers to be team captains and ask them in turn to pick their team members. Shuffle the pictures and cards, pick out a picture at random and show it to everyone. Pick out three letters at random from the alphabet set and a plus or minus symbol.

Explain that the idea of the game is for the teams to come up with as many words as possible starting with the given letters which describe the person in the picture. If the symbol is a plus symbol, then all the words are to be positive. If the symbol that you have chosen is a minus, then all the words are to be negative.

Give them one minute to do this. Check their answers and award one point for every correct word that each team has. Play several rounds of the game. The winning team is the one with the most points at the end of the given time.

Commentator

2 minutes

"We can place a great importance on how people react to us and what people say about us. How would the people you were describing in the Countdown game feel if they heard your descriptions of them? People's reactions and comments can make us feel good about ourselves; other times they can have the adverse affect.

Some we may forget, but some reactions stick with us. These are usually the negative ones which can cause us to feel quite sad about ourselves. But do the reactions and comments of others give us a correct picture of ourselves?"

LAP 2

Thought: God's picture of us

Total Time: 20 minutes

The shepherd drive

15 minutes

REW Split the group into teams.
Form groups around the room by taking one person from each team and placing them with one member from each of the other teams. Give each person a copy of the activity sheet (page 22) and some scissors. Ask each member to cut out the seven pieces of the shepherd's body. Give each group a dice and play as follows:

Each of the shepherd pieces are numbered. On their turn a player rolls the die, finds the matching numbered shepherd piece and places it in front of them. In subsequent throws the players are to try and bring all the other pieces into play and therefore construct the shepherd (two number sixes are needed to get both feet). If a player rolls a number which matches a numbered piece they already have, then they cannot add a piece to their shepherd and must pass the die to the next person in their group. The winner of each group is the one who constructs their shepherd first. Discover who is the winner of each group and ask them which team they are in. See which team at the end has the most group winners.

The group members may well want to play this game more than once. To make it more difficult, you could ask the players to look up the Bible verse indicated on each piece as they win it, and write it down. The winner of each group is then the one who has a complete shepherd with all the Bible verses written legibly.

Commentator

5 minutes

"A shepherd's role in Jesus' day was perhaps more understood and appreciated by his audience than it is in today's society. However the picture of a shepherd is a very useful one if we are to know how God views each one of us.

A shepherd was responsible for his master's sheep: he guided them to good grazing land, cared for their well-being, protected them and provided all that they needed. In calling himself the Good Shepherd Jesus was saying that all these qualities and more could be found in him. Jesus takes such an interest in us because we are unique, precious and valuable to him. Read Luke 15:4–7.

We've seen that it's very easy to judge ourselves on what others think and say about us. Christians believe that if we want to know what our true worth is, then we should listen to Jesus."

Thought: God can make a difference to your personal view of yourself

LAP 3

Total Time: 33 minutes

An interactive story

31 minutes

REW Tell the story of Jesus meeting the Samaritan woman, found in John 4:5–30, but making it interactive by stopping at the appropriate points and interjecting the activities below. Be ready to move on quickly to ensure the story does not drag.

Jesus was tired (verse 6)
Activity 1

A challenge which will make the participants tire quickly eg, holding both arms outstretched at shoulder height with a book in each hand, or holding a heavy object above their head without moving. Anyone who moves is out.

Jesus gave her an opportunity (verse 10)
Activity 2 *(2 minutes)*

Display John 4:13,14 written out as follows and see who can be the first person to discover what it says:-

Jesusansweredwhoeverdrinksthiswaterwillbethirsty
againbutwhoeverdrinksthewaterthatiwillgivehimwill
neverbethirstyagainthewaterthatiwillgivehimwillbec

omeinhimaspringwhichwillprovidehimwithlifegivin
gwaterandgivehimeternallife.

Jesus asked an embarrassing question (verse 15)
Activity 3 *(2 minutes)*

Find out the most embarrassing moment that your group members have ever experienced.

The woman asked a hard question (verse 19)
Activity 4 *(2 minutes)*

Find out who may have a good religious-sounding question eg, something you would ask a bishop or the Pope.

Activity 5 *(1 minute)*

Split the group into teams and see which one can produce the longest list of places where you may be able to worship God.

Jesus shared privileged information (verse 26)
Activity 6 *(1 minute)*

Have the following written out on a card and see if anyone can work it out. (Read backwards for the answers.)

uoy htiw gniklat si ohw eh ma I derewsna suseJ

Surprised reactions (verse 27)
Activity 7 *(2 minutes)*

See which group member can pull the most effective surprised facial expression.

Commentator   *2 minutes*

"If you were in the woman's position, isolated and seen as unclean by other people of the town, how would you feel about yourself? The likelihood is that you would have a negative view of yourself.

Jesus showed this woman that she was important and valuable to God by revealing that she could know God for herself and worship him in her heart and that it was through him, Jesus, that all these things are possible.

He showed her that she was loved and cared for when everyone else was perhaps saying the opposite. This knowledge transformed her. Instead of avoiding people she actively went around sharing her wonderful discovery of Jesus with others."

Chequered Flag   8 minutes

Read Matthew 7:7–11. We all need to know that we are valued, loved and cared for. Often we try to gauge our worth by the comments and reactions of others to ourselves. As a result we may get an inconsistent and incorrect impression of ourselves. God, however, is consistent in his view of us. He always loves us. In fact we are so precious to him that he was even willing to die on our behalf!

On the Podium   5 minutes

Award prizes for the following activities: Valuable or not?, Countdown, The shepherd drive and the Interactive story activities 1–10.

Lap of Honour   10 minutes

Play some background meditative music. Read Psalm 139:1–18 to the group. Explain that this is a wonderful psalm illustrating just how much God knows, cares and loves us. Ask them to write down on a piece of paper all the activities they have done (in order) up to this particular point in the day.

Once people have done this, ask them to go quietly through each activity on their list and repeat verse 7b ('Where could I get away from your presence?') after each one listed, as well as thanking God for his constant love and care. Finish with a closing prayer.

Success or failure

Qualifying

So much importance is placed upon being a success in our world today that we can lose sight of what God wants from us: to be faithful followers of him. This session seeks to contrast the world's and God's view of success, encouraging the members to seek to be a success in God's eyes above anything else.

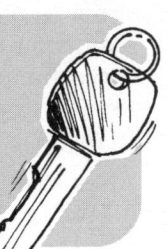

Starting Grid
(up to 20 minutes)

Ⓐ Pop star picture quiz — 10 minutes

Buy some young people's magazines with posters of pop stars in. Mount the A4 posters on card. Cut each poster into 5 pieces and number each piece 1 to 5. Split your group into two teams. For each team's turn ask them to select a number between 1 and 5 (hide the pieces from view), then show them the selected piece. They must try and correctly identify the person/pop group. If they have no idea, ask the same team to select another piece and so on until they answer correctly. Do the same for the next team. Have enough posters prepared so that each team can have about four rounds. Decrease points scored with each extra piece they are shown eg, by 10 points for the first piece shown, down to 2 points if all are shown.

Ⓑ 'Who am I?' quiz — 10 minutes

This is similar to the above quiz, but instead of pictures, use five facts about well known media stars. Again, such facts can be obtained from young people's magazines. Split the group into two teams and play as above.

Ⓒ Impossible tasks — up to 20 minutes

Pick some activities from the *Guinness Book of Records* and see if any group member can beat the record set. Obviously most will fail, giving you a link into the issue of failure. For example, discover who can eat the most cold baked beans with a cocktail stick in 1 minute. Multiply the score by 30 and find out what total you get. See how near it comes to the record set by Karen Stevenson of Merseyside who ate 2,780 in 30 minutes (1997 edition)!

Commentator

1 minute

"Today we are looking at the subject of success and failure, experiences that we will all face in life, to a greater or lesser degree."

Thought:
What are the things that society believes makes a successful person?

Total Time: 30 minutes

Ⓐ Caricatures — 20 minutes

Working in pairs, ask the group to produce a caricature of what they would say a successful person looked like and the particular characteristics that they would possess. Have available the appropriate materials to make a cartoon drawing, a dough/plasticine model or a figure carved from a bar of soap.

Commentator

3 minutes

"Ask the group members to explain their caricatures and what they felt were the key things which makes somebody successful.

Make a list of these characteristics. One might expect such answers as qualifications, job, money, income, great appearance etc. Explain that you would like them to think about which characteristics they consider to be the most important for success."

B What's more important?

6 minutes

Split the group into teams and supply each team with an identical length of wallpaper. Ask them to list the characteristics in order of priority and then divide the area of wallpaper up graphically representing their importance, ie the most important items get a greater amount of space than the least important items.

After each team has completed this exercise, place all the lengths of wallpaper side by side. Ask each team to explain the reasons for their answers and then compare results.

Commentator

1 minute

"As we have just discovered, people have different thoughts as to what makes a person successful and which characteristics are the most important. Given such thoughts, how successful would you consider yourself to be?"

we then form a judgement about ourselves. However, is the judgement we form a true and fair one? Are we a failure/valuable if we don't do well in exams? Are we a failure/valuable if we haven't got lots of money and the latest fashion items?

Sometimes we may think we are a failure, but the Bible encourages us by telling us two important facts:

Firstly we are valuable to God for simply being who we are, not for what we do or what we look like, and secondly, according to the Bible, whether we are a success or a failure is dependent on something else other than education, appearance, job, money, etc."

Thought:
How successful do you feel?

Total Time: 9 minutes

Thought:
Who does God regard as successful people?

Total Time: up to 17 minutes

The wise and foolish house builders (Matthew 7:24–27)

15 minutes

'How do you feel?' survey

7 minutes

Give one copy of the survey (see page 26) to each person. Ask them to fill it in, according to the instructions given, as honestly as possible.

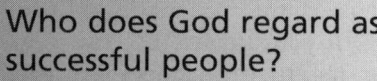 You could just read the story and go on to the commentator section below or, if you want to explore the story and its meaning further, choose one of the following methods:-

a) Story rewrite

Read the passage to the group and then try and get the group members to think about modern day equivalents to this story. For example, a modern equivalent of 'anyone who hears these words of mine and obeys them is like...', could be 'someone who does plenty of revision before taking an exam' or 'someone who reads the Highway code before taking a driving test'.

Commentator

2 minutes

"As there is so much pressure in our society for us to be a success, in order to try and reassure ourselves that we are successful, we might do three things:

• We might STOP and compare ourselves with those around us.

• We might LOOK at what society says makes somebody successful.

• We might LISTEN to the comments other people say about us.

From these comparisons and comments

Then split them into groups to devise a sketch based around such modern day equivalents. Discuss how their ideas relate to Jesus' idea of success, ie a person is successful in God's sight if they hear and obey his words. Make sure that they understand the principles of the parable.

Commentator
2 minutes

"By telling this story Jesus was emphasising that those whom God deems successful in life are those who choose to build their lives on his word and be obedient to it. How well do we measure up?

Some may feel complete failures when measured up to God's requirements, but the good news is that God helps us in our weakness."

Thought:
Jesus helping us through failure
Total Time: upto 31 minutes

Identification parade
10 minutes

Choose one group member and blindfold him. Then choose a selection of other group members to take it in turns to do one of the following activities close to the blindfolded person, eg scream, gargle a tune, blow a raspberry, make a noise like a monkey, cow, sheep etc.

They then all line up and the blindfolded member has to choose the culprit out of the line, with their blindfold removed. Repeat until all who want a turn have been blindfolded.

Explain that the blindfolded members weren't completely sure about who the true culprit was. Read Matthew 26:69–75. When Jesus had been arrested, Peter was sitting in a courtyard waiting to see what would become of Jesus. While he was there, three people on three separate occasions positively identified Peter as being one of Jesus' disciples. Peter felt very pressured by this and, even though he had known Jesus for three years, denied three times that he ever knew him!

Commentator
2 minutes

"Jesus had foretold this event to Peter, but Peter had dismissed the idea as totally unthinkable, in fact he said that even though it may mean dying, he would never say such a thing (Matthew 26:35). Yet despite what he said and despite being one of Jesus' strongest followers, he still denied Jesus. He failed to stand up for Jesus, his friend, even when he needed him most. He realised what Jesus had foretold had come true, and we read that he was absolutely devastated and left that place weeping bitterly. Peter – one of Jesus' strongest followers – had failed him! We're in good company if we know that we've failed God."

Chattabox video clip
10 minutes

If you have a younger group, show the relevant clip from this SU video. Prepare some observation questions to ask about it afterwards.

Commentator
8 minutes

"Although Peter had failed Jesus, Jesus didn't give up on him. Instead he came alongside him, forgave him and gave him the strength to follow him once more. We all fail Jesus again and again by not living for him 100% of the time, yet it is wonderful to know that Jesus will do the same for us as he did for Peter: he'll come alongside us, forgive us and help us live for him once more."

Chequered Flag
5 minutes

Society often judges how successful people are by their qualifications, job, income, possessions, appearance and many other things. In God's eyes a successful person is someone who chooses to follow him and obey his word. There will be times when those who try to follow God will fail, just like Peter did. However it's wonderful to know that when we fail, Jesus is there to pick us up, forgive us and help us on the right way again.

We need to make a decision, though: are we wanting to find success primarily in the world's eyes or in God's eyes?

On the Podium
2 minutes
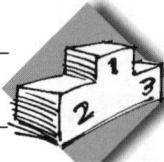

Award the prizes for the following activities: *Pop star quiz*, *'Who am I?' quiz* and *Impossible tasks*.

How successful are you? survey

Place one of the following symbols in the space provided in each statement indicating how successful you feel in each case. Then give yourself a general score out of 10 in the space provided.

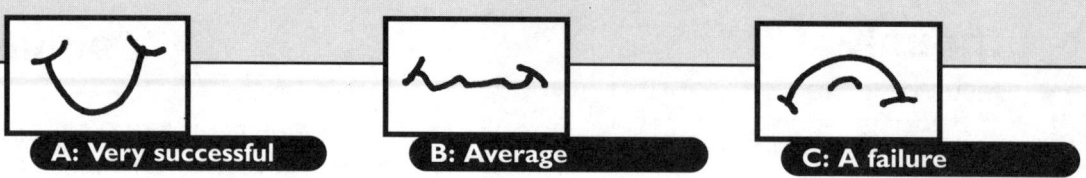

A: Very successful   **B: Average**   **C: A failure**

❶ I feel that I am .... academically – look at my exam results!!

❷ I feel that I am .... athletically – look at my sprint time.

❸ I feel that I am .... at forming relationships with the opposite sex.

❹ My bodily appearance makes me feel .... – see how people treat me.

❺ My possessions make me feel .... – see how people react to them.

❻ My clothes make me feel .... – see how people talk.

❼ My popularity makes me feel .... – see how many friends I have!!

❽ My relationship with my parents makes me feel .... – how many times do we fight?

❾ The money I receive makes me feel .... – look what I can buy.

❿ I believe that the skills I am learning now will allow me to be .... in the future.

```
I FEEL
A GREAT
FAILURE

1
2
3
4
5
6
7
8
9
10

I FEEL
A GREAT
SUCCESS
```

ACTIVITY SHEET

Searching for Riches

Qualifying

Materialism and the drive to have more is all too prevalent in our society, affecting members of all generations. This session seeks to challenge the group members to become rich in God's sight, to strive for eternal riches rather than placing too much importance upon material possessions.

I recommend that you attempt 'The pearl game' in Lap 1, although it may sound complicated, it isn't. It's an excellent way of introducing the issue of materialism. It could be used instead of a Starting Grid activity.

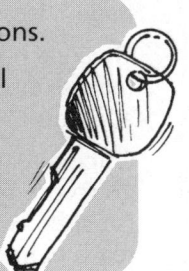

Starting Grid
(up to 10 minutes)

A Money grab

10 minutes

Warning: This game may not be appropriate for girls wearing skirts!!

Before you start, mark a two-metre diameter circle on the floor using some tape. Also prepare strips of thin paper, tissue or foil (the more the better) to represent bank notes. Arrange a minimum of five group members around the edge of the circle facing outwards, legs apart, with their heels touching the tape. Ask these players to then bend over (Group A).

Select other group members to then stand facing them and give them all a supply of bank notes (Group B). On a given signal Group B are to throw, waft and blow these notes over Group A and into the centre of the circle.

Group A are then to reach for these notes through their legs, without moving into the circle. They are to collect as many notes as possible within 1 minute or until all the notes have been used up. The winner is the one with the most notes collected.

Collect the paper up once more and swap the roles of the group members so that everyone has a chance of playing each part.

Vary this game by adding different coloured bank notes, some of which could stand for illegal tender and therefore can't be counted!

B Coin balance

6 minutes

Split the group into twos or threes and supply them with a pile of coins. See which team can build the highest tower of coins on their team-mate's forehead!

C Jar count

3 minutes

Place as much loose change in a jar as possible and see if anyone can guess the total amount contained within, in pounds/pence.

D Make a currency

10 minutes

In small teams ask the group to design and make a series of imaginary bank notes. Award prizes for different categories eg, design, colour, usability etc.

Thought:
To demonstrate materialism

Total Time: up to 40 minutes

LAP 1

The pearl game

30 minutes

a) Part 1

Jelly bean swap

Split the group into teams and give each member in the team a coloured jelly bean, handing them out randomly. Explain that the winning team is the team who can swap all their beans with another in order to try and obtain the most beans of the same colour.

Give five extra beans (randonmly selected) to the winning team.

b) Part 2

Game instructions

Explain that each of the beans that the team has collected represents money, the amounts of which vary according to their colour.

Display the first list of values (see over). Explain that during the course of the game these values will change.

The idea of the game is very simple: they are to buy

as many expensive top quality pearls as possible from the jewellers. If they cannot afford any of these pearls then they are to do certain tasks in order to get some more random beans from the bank manager. The more tasks a team completes, the more pearls they can buy. (For list of tasks see page 30.)

Give each team a task sheet, then explain that the teams only have a set time ie 15–20 minutes, to accumulate their wealth.

Once a team feels they have completed a task they go to the bank manager who examines their finished work and signs their task sheet so that the team cannot do the same task twice. Depending on how well that task was achieved and the amount of jelly beans the task could possibly be worth, the bank manager decides how many beans to give to the team (see page 30).

At the end of the game any remaining beans which have not been converted to pearls will not be counted!

Practical details for the leader

You need at least one person to be a jeweller, where each team can exchange their beans for pearls, and at least one bank manager.

The jeweller will need a supply of pearls (circles of paper each marked with a value between twenty pounds and one hundred pounds).

After every five minutes change the value of beans to the following:

	Original	Change 1	Change 2	Change 3
Red	£5	10p	£1	£3
Orange	£4	50p	50p	£5
Green	£3	£2	£3	50p
Yellow	£2	£1	£5	£4
Black	£1	£4	10p	£2
White	50p	£3	£4	10p
Pink	10p	£5	£2	£1

In order for the teams to complete the tasks provide some Bibles, scrap paper, newspaper, scissors, pens, pencils and crayons.

Be strict on time and rules. At the end find out which team won and award points accordingly.

Commentator

10 minutes

" Find out from the group members:

a) how they felt when they saw their beans and heard how much they were worth.

b) what their reaction was to their situation, ie Did they give up or work hard?

This simulation game reflected some important facts that we face in life:

- Not everyone had the same amount of money/wealth at the beginning and during the game due to differing circumstances.

- People coped with this situation in different ways. Some were determined to do their best in order to buy the pearls at no matter what cost, while others perhaps were not as enthusiastic.

Ask if any of the group members are desperately wanting a particular item at the moment and if so what they have been prepared to do to raise money to buy it.

Use Bible passages to explain that everything in this world is God's (Psalm 50:12; 1 Corinthians 10:26) and that he generously gives us wealth to use wisely and enjoy (Ecclesiastes 5:19). However, he doesn't want our wealth and possessions to become the main focus of our attention. We may lose sight of what really matters in life (1 Timothy 6:9,10). "

Thought:

What really matters in life?

Total Time: 13 minutes

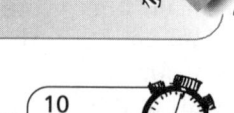

Fools' gold worksheet

10 minutes

Photocopy the activity sheet on page 31. This is based on the parable of the rich fool found in Luke 12:13–21. After a while go through the story so that everyone knows the correct answers.

Commentator

3 minutes

" In the story we hear about a man who wanted to store up more and more things for himself so that he could take it easy and enjoy himself. God himself called this man a fool. Why? This man had made his wealth the focus of attention. He was to discover that his wealth was only valid on earth and didn't make him rich in God's eyes. He should have placed his focus of attention upon the things of God which would have made him rich in God's eyes and rich for all eternity! "

LAP 3

Thought:
Storing up treasure that will last
Total Time: 20 minutes

Treasure verse (15 minutes)

Prepare cards with the following words and numbers on, so that when collected the respective verses can be made. (Matthew 6:19–21).

Bible verse A

Do(4) / not store(11) / up riches(7) / for yourselves(12) / here on(3) / earth(10), / where moths(1) / and rust(5) / destroy and(8) / robbers break(6) / in and(9) / steal(2).

Bible verse B

Instead(16) / store up(19) / riches for(24) / yourselves in(13) / heaven(20) / where moths(15) / and rust(18) / cannot destroy(22) / and robbers(17) / cannot break(23) / in and(14) / steal(21).

Combination verse

For(25) / your(26) / heart(27) / will(28) / always(29) / be(30) / where(31) / your(32) / riches(33) / are(34).

Copy the master game board (see page 32). Have available (for your eyes only) the grid below which reveals where each part of the verses are hidden, eg A1 equals card 25 of the combination verse.

F	3A	24B	Miss a turn	4A	34C	28C	6A
E	21B	10A	18B	31C	27C	20B	12A
D	8A	Another turn	2A	19B	Another turn	32C	Miss a turn
C	15B	29C	1A	26C	9A	7A	22B
B	23B	11A	Miss a turn	17B	Another turn	14B	33C
A	25C	Miss a turn	13B	30C	5A	Another turn	16B
	1	2	3	4	5	6	7

Game instructions

Split the group into two teams, A and B. Explain that the idea of the game is to choose grid references in order to try and obtain all the pieces to make up their team Bible verse ie Team A = Bible verse A, Team B = Bible verse B. The first team to receive and make up their verse wins 10 points.

They need to choose references wisely because they may choose a grid reference which contains a piece of the opposing teams Bible verse, and if they do that then the opposing team automatically receives that piece and then has their turn.

They may find a piece of the combination verse. If they do, then the team who chooses it receives points equalling the amount of letters of the word contained on the card. Place the piece in the middle of the two teams.

Also explain that some grid references when chosen may mean a team either missing a turn or having another go.

The team with the most points wins.

Commentator
5 minutes

"Jesus encourages us to store treasures in heaven, those which will last for all eternity. What does that mean? Jesus wants us to place importance on the things that we can do on earth which have eternal consequences. These things include:

a) choosing to have a friendship with Jesus as he is the source of eternal life (John 14:60)

b) working with the Holy Spirit to produce in ourselves a Christ-like character / godliness (1 Timothy 4:6–10);

c) using our money to help achieve God's purposes in the world (2 Corinthians 9)."

Chequered Flag   5 minutes

Finish by reading Matthew 13:44–46. Here are two instances where a man was willing to give up/sell everything he had in order to gain that of great value. We all have a tendency of wanting more wealth/possessions in our life, but how willing are we to lay this desire aside and put God first in our lives so that we may gain from him a friendship and riches, that promise to last for all eternity?

On the Podium   2 minutes

Award prizes for *The pearl game* and *Treasure verse*.

Lap of Honour   10 minutes

Obtain a copy of Iona's album *Beyond these shores*, and play the track 'Treasure'. The chorus 'Where you treasure is, there is your heart' sums up the session.

Play it with just the words on view or play while showing a previously recorded TV game show with the sound turned down. (The clip could show, for example, someone winning a fortune or the lottery draw.) Use it as a basis to thank God that he can be trusted to look after his friends.

Pearl TASKS Game

Activity Sheet 5a

Complete the tasks below in order to get further jelly beans. Show your completed tasks and collect your beans from the bank manager. Exchange beans for pearls at the jewellers as soon as possible as any beans not converted to pearls will not be counted when time is up!

	TASK	JELLY BEANS	SIGNATURE
1	Draw three pictures illustrating three parables that Jesus told.	1–2	
2	On paper name six disciples of Jesus.	1–2	
3	List ten qualities that you feel Jesus has.	1–2	
4	List ten books of the Bible.	1–2	
5	List five miracles that Jesus did.	1–2	
6	Make a donkey that Jesus may have ridden.	1–2	
7	As a group sing a song about Jesus.	1–2	
8	If Jesus had a car, what do you think it would be?	1–2	
9	Make two team members into animals from the Bible.	1–2	
10	Jesus is often called the servant king. Draw a cartoon of this.	1–2	
11	List ten things that you look for in a friend.	1–2	
12	Which one question would each team member ask Jesus?	1–2	
13	Form ten new words from 'A forgiver of wrong'.	1–2	
14	Make the number of coins that Jesus was betrayed for.	1–2	
15	Draw a picture of how you picture God.	2–3	
16	Jesus is the Good Shepherd – all become noisy sheep.	2–3	
17	Ask ten people how they are, then collect their signatures.	2–3	
18	Draw something Jesus might have made as a carpenter.	2–3	
19	Draw a picture of what heaven might be like.	2–3	
20	Recreate the scene of Jesus feeding the 5000.	2–3	
21	Read Matthew 1:1–6 without stumbling.	2–3	
22	As a team, laugh uncontrollably for one minute.	2–3	
23	Draw three pictures illustrating three parables that Jesus told.	2–3	
24	Make a poster advertising Jesus to your friends.	3–4	
25	Make a boat you think Jesus might have travelled in.	3–4	
26	What would your definition of love be?	3–4	
27	Recreate the nativity scene as a group.	3–4	
28	Build a 3D model of a church.	3–4	
29	Find out what 'Emmanuel' means.	3–4	
30	Peter and John were fishermen. Make a rod with twelve fish on it.	4–5	
31	Jesus did miracles. Step *through* an A4 piece of paper.	4–5	

FOOLS' Gold

5b

Fit the following words in the grid to complete the story and reveal the secret which will help you complete the maze successfully.

all	bigger	crops	easy	fool	give
Gods	good	kept	lucky	many	rich
riches	tear	these	things	think	will
will	yourself	yourself			

There was once a				man
who had land which bore				crops
He began to				to himself
I haven't anywhere to keep all my				what can I do?
I will				down my barns
and build				ones
where I will store my crops and				my other gods
then I				say to myself
				man
you have all the good				
you need for				years
take life				
eat, drink and enjoy				
But God said to him "You				
this very night you				
have to				up your life
then who will get all				
things you have				for
This is how it is for those who pile				up
for themselves but are not rich in				sight

Work your way through the maze only passing through the doors with the handle on your side. As you pass capital letters note them down to find out why Jesus told us to avoid all kinds of greed.

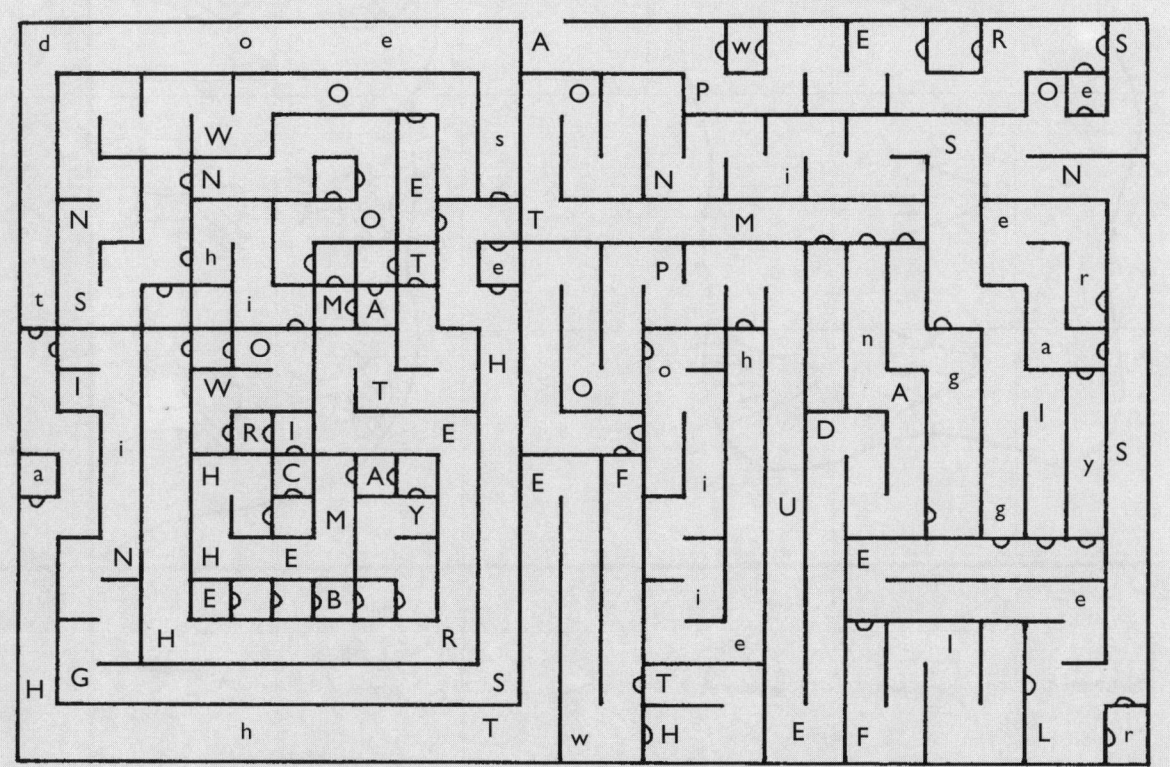

ACTIVITY SHEET

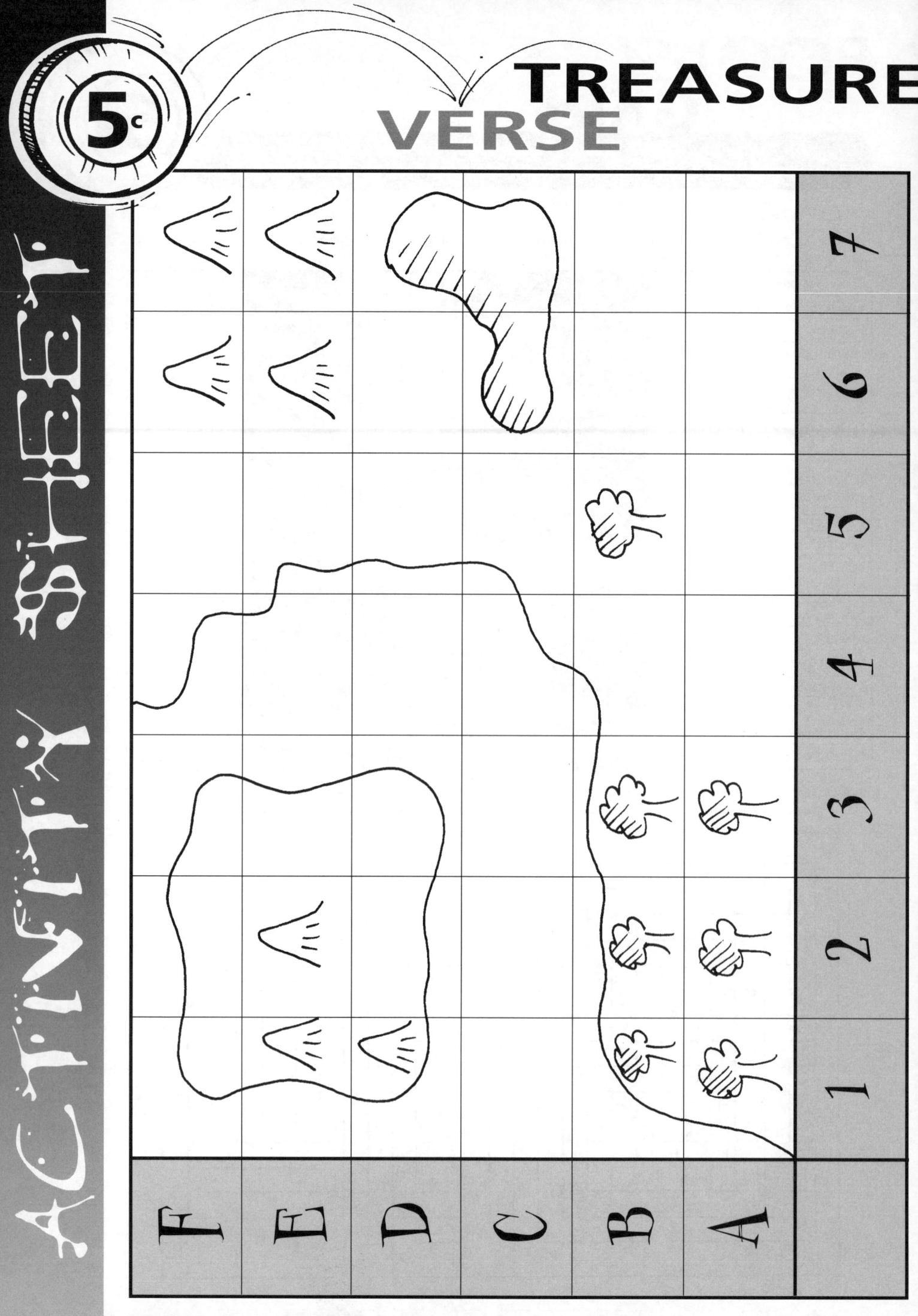

Families

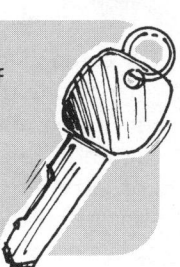

Qualifying

You will need to tackle this subject quite sensitively as young people within your group may have had either positive or negative experiences of family life. The reality of family problems is explored and group members are encouraged to seek the love and support of God, the perfect parent.

Starting Grid
(7 minutes minimum)

Ⓐ Family quiz — 20 minutes

Similar to a TV game show.

Split the group into two teams. Pick one player from each team to play against each other to answer a question eg:

Name five excuses for not doing the washing up
1 It's not my turn to do it
2 We've got a dishwasher
3 I'm allergic to washing-up liquid
4 We've no washing-up liquid left
5 My arms are tired

Ask the question and the first player (of the two picked) to put up his hand gets to answer first. Compare the answer with your lists. If the answer is not the top of your list then ask the other contestant for his answer. Whoever gives the most popular answers has a choice to either play or pass.

If they choose to play, then the team has to try to guess all the answers on the list They are allowed to have two wrong guesses, after which the other team has one turn only to find one of the missing answers. If they do, then they win that round. If they choose to pass, then they wait to guess any missing answers to the question as described above. Play the best of three rounds. Create your own survey for the following topics: things that parents moan at their children for; times when a family insists on being together; things that parents do to embarrass their children.

Ⓑ Groupings — 6 minutes

Write up a list of animal species and another of the collective nouns used to describe them. See which team member/pairing can identify the most animal group names correctly eg, a pride of lions, a herd of cattle, a litter of pups.

Commentator — 1 minute

"Families exist in many different forms, but we all have expectations as to how members within it should behave."

Thought:
Understanding family roles
Total Time: up to 30 minutes

Design an advert — 10 minutes

Give each member paper and a pen. Ask each group member to design an advert for the perfect parent that could go into a newspaper or magazine, which outlines the key qualities and role that they would want a parent to have. Ask each member to read out their advert and if possible to give a reason why they think their chosen qualities are important in a parent.

Commentator — 1 minute

"Unfortunately our parents will never totally fulfil these roles. God shows in the Bible how he expects parents to behave."

The parent challenge — 5 minutes

Make two copies of a simple figure and then draw six boxes within them. Write one of the following expectations on each box:
1 Parents are to teach their children how to live (Proverbs 22:6).
2 Parents are to correct their children (Proverbs 13:24).
3 Parents are to provide for their children (2 Corinthians 12:14).

4 Parents are to control their children (1 Timothy 3:4).
5 Parents are to teach their children about God (Deuteronomy 6:7).
6 Parents are not to provoke their children to anger (Ephesians 6:4).

Cover each statement with a numbered card. Divide into two teams, each with a copy of the figure and a die. Each team member takes a turn to throw the die and then open the numbered window corresponding to their score. If there is no card of that number, or if it is already open, pass on to the next person. The winning team is the first to reveal all of the statements.

Compare the biblical parent expectations with their previously stated perfect parent qualities.

Read an advert  8 minutes

Make copies of the advertisement on page 36. Explain that in the publication for which group members wrote their adverts for the perfect parents, this advert was spotted.

Ask each member to read and mark those qualities which the Bible encourages and expects children within a family to possess. Answers:
Proverbs 20:11 (3), Psalm 34:11 (4), Ecclesiastes 12:1 (8), Ephesians 6:1 (13), Colossians 3:20 (13), Exodus 20:12 (15)

Ask the group whether or not they agree with these expectations. Are they unrealistic? Why do they think that the Bible encourages such behaviour in children?

Commentator
up to 5 minutes

"God expects the family to be a place of mutual love, support, learning and growth. To achieve this, God gives each member of the family guidance as to their role within it. Unfortunately, things can go wrong."

Thought: A family in crisis
Total Time: up to 25 minutes

Crime watch reconstruction (Genesis 27)

Split the group into teams. Take the role of a detective. Explain to your fellow officers (the group members) that recent reports have suggested that a man by the name of Jacob tricked his dying father into giving him the headship of his family and estate, which should have rightfully belonged to his older brother, Esau. The outcome of this is that Esau is now looking to kill his brother Jacob. The information received is as follows:

Information
There are four characters involved in the incident, of which we know the following facts:

Isaac: He was the father and the head of the family.
He was partial to a nice meat dish.
He was blind and was probably on his deathbed when this incident occurred.
He wanted to pass over the headship of the family and all his estate to his favoured eldest son, Esau, before he died.

Rebecca: She was Isaac's wife, and a good cook.
Her favourite son was Jacob.
She had been known to eavesdrop.

Esau: He was the eldest son, whose name means hairy.
He was a skilled hunter and loved to spend his time out in the fields.

Jacob: He was the youngest son, a quiet man who usually stayed at home with the tents.
He made a very nice vegetable soup.
Before this incident occurred, he had already obtained the rights that Esau had as the firstborn son.

Explain that they are to examine the information/facts of the case, then try and reconstruct the event and the events proceeding it, in order to try and determine what actually happened.

How did Jacob know that his father was going to bless Esau? How did he trick his father? What role did Rebecca and Esau have?

Give the teams sufficient time to look at the information and try and reconstruct the events which led up to and which happened during Jacob's deception.

Allow each team to perform their version of events to the other teams.

Finish off by explaining what really happened. (See Genesis 25:27–34; 27:1–45.)

Commentator
 2 minutes

"Instead of a mutual love and respect for each other, we see that other qualities had crept into this family.

Favouritism was shown by both parents towards a different son. Which resulted in jealousy, deception and a lack of trust between them.

God is saddened by such events. However, he does provide a way for us all to

> experience a new level of love, strength and security through a relationship with him, the perfect parent. One thing that we can be totally sure of is that he won't let us down! "

Thought:
God is our father

Total Time: up to 18 minutes

God, the perfect parent

up to 15 minutes

Before the game, prepare a set of all the letters used in the answers to the questions below. Stick them up at random all around the meeting room. Split the group into teams.

Give your group Bibles and read Hosea 11.

Ask each team in turn to choose a number between 1–11 corresponding to a Bible verse and question. The teams each compete to construct the answer to their question by collecting the letters displayed around the room. Award points for the first correct answer brought forward.

Questions

- v 1) What is the word which means a male offspring?   SON
- v 2) What is the word which means to speak loudly so as to attract attention?   CALLED
- v 3) What is the word God uses to describe how he looks after his people?   CARE
- v 4) What word describes God's tender love for his people?   AFFECTION
- v 5) What word describes Israel's choice of rejecting God's love and support?   REFUSE
- v 6) Who were the Israelites trying to please?   THEMSELVES
- v 7) What word describes Israel's determined demand to turn away from God?   INSIST
- v 8) Why doesn't God abandon his people?   LOVE
- v 9) What quality does God say that he would not punish Israel in?   ANGER
- v 10) What does God, expect his people to do, and means to go after?   FOLLOW
- v 11) Where will God bring his people to again, their?   HOMES

Commentator

3 minutes

" God is pictured like a parent to Israel, his special chosen people. We can almost feel God's disappointment and distress, as he sees his loved ones heading straight for hard times. However, he doesn't abandon his people, but sticks with them, waiting for the day when they will turn back to him once more.

In the passage, God was speaking to his nation Israel, but we can also know God as our Father for ourselves. In effect we can become adopted into his family. This is made possible through Jesus (John 1:12). "

Chequered Flag   5 minutes

God is committed to the family and sees it as an important place of mutual love, support, learning and growth. Even if our own family suffers hardship/breakdown, God is so good that he provides a way through Jesus in which we can have a relationship with him and know him as our perfect heavenly Father. It is only when we become a member of God's family that we find the level of love and support that we all desperately crave.

On the Podium   5 minutes

Award prizes for the following: *Family quiz, Groupings, The parent challenge* and *God, the perfect parent.*

Lap of Honour   10 minutes

Find the words to the song, 'Father God I Wonder' by Ian Smale. Sing this song with your group or play some instrumental music in the background and ask them to read the words of the hymn carefully. Ask them to draw something which symbolises how they feel about the Father's love portrayed in the song. (Explain that these drawings won't have to be displayed around the group.)

WANTED
for some have-a-go parents

A YOUNG PERSON WHO WILL:

1 Bring breakfast in bed every morning
2 Always be bright and pleasant in character
3 Be wise in their understanding and behaviour
4 Listen to the concerns of their parents
5 Not play loud music
6 Not have any of their body pierced
7 Always do their homework
8 Remember to follow and worship God
9 Have a sense of humour
10 Get a job to help with the house expenses
11 Not demand pocket money
12 Loves to give rather than receive
13 Obey all instructions given
14 Always get on with their friends
15 Honour and respect each parent

Reply to Mr and Mrs Pigsmight Fly

Friends

Qualifying

Friends become increasingly important to the developing young person, as they seek to find a sense of identity, security and acceptance in their age of change. However, as they learn to relate to more young people of their age, they will experience both successful and unsuccessful friendships with people. This session seeks to explore the qualities which make good friendships, before looking at the example and teachings of Jesus and Paul.

Starting Grid
(up to 10 minutes)

A No hands

10 minutes

Pick four volunteers. Ask two of them to place their hands behind their back and ask the other two to stand behind them, threading their arms through those of the volunteers in front of them, so that the back volunteers provide the arms to the volunteers in front of them.

Stand them all in front of a table with many different cosmetic products on. Explain that both pairs are friends shopping for cometics/make-up and are trying different products on. Ask them to then act out the scene using the provided items.

Other scenarios that you could have other volunteers acting out: two friends helping each other bake a cake in school (provide baking materials) or two friends chatting and eating their lunch at school (provide food).

B Self disclosure

8 minutes

Place people into pairs and ask each person within the group to write five things about themselves that others may not necessarily know. Label each person in a pair either A or B. Give person A 30 seconds to talk to their partner B about themselves whilst including their five written facts. Their partner B then has 20 seconds to try and name all the facts that partner A has written on their paper. See how many they name. Swap roles and then repeat.

Thought:
Encouraging the group members to think how good they may be as a friend.

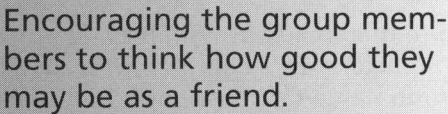

Total Time: 21 minutes

What sort of friend are you?

10 minutes

Copy sufficient numbers of the activity sheet (see page 40) so that every member has a copy. Ask them to work through the various options in order to arrive at A, B, C or D.

Explain that the activity sheet only gives a loose indication of how they relate to their friends. Read the following descriptions, which relate to boxes A, B, C or D, wait for any responses and move on to the next activity.

Friend type A

It seems that you would do anything for a friend, even lie on their behalf, no matter what the cost may be to yourself. Although this loyalty is very commendable it could lead you into situations that you would rather not be in. Try to avoid just having one good friend – you would benefit by having several.

Friend type B

You seem to have a sensible and honest head on your shoulders, someone who will give and take in a friendship, someone who would be a real pleasure to know. Keep on making wise choices!

Friend type C

You seem to want friendships but on your terms – after all, you like being in control of your life. Try not to view potential friends suspiciously and learn to trust others more. Try to put more effort into the friends that you have, learning to give of yourself to others with a happier heart so that you will see people warm to you

Friend type D

Friends to you at this time may not be important, but I assure you that they will become more of an issue to you as you grow older. So, if you don't want to be left on your own in the future, make friends now and try and give as much to people as you take. After all friends that you make now may well stay friends with you for a lifetime.

Friendship outburst

 Split the group into two teams and ask them both to write down:

a) as many qualities as they can which they think make a really good friend;

b) as many qualities as they can which they think make a really bad friend.

Ask each team to then read out both lists, to see how the differing teams' lists compare with each other. Ask them to name the most important quality they require in a friend.

Commentator

1 minute

" We all need to have friends, people we can relate to and share our lives with. Friendships are often the source of great happiness but likewise can also be the source of great sadness when either we hurt our friends or they hurt us. We therefore need to be aware of the qualities that ensure friendships last. Many of the qualities already mentioned are very commendable, but how do they match up with those qualities that we are encouraged to possess through the teaching of the Bible? "

Thought:
The extent of Jesus' love for his friends

Total Time: up to 26 minutes

Card quiz

 Write out John 15:12,13 with each of the words of the verse on a separate card. On the reverse write a number, corresponding with the position the word comes in the verse. For example 'commandment' will be number 2 and 'friends' will be number 22, using the GNB.

Place the cards in order on a board, with the numbers facing the group members. Split the group into teams. On their turn each team chooses a number. Turn over the number to reveal the word. Award the teams points corresponding to the number of letters the word has in it. For example 'commandment' will be worth 11 points and 'friends' will be worth 7 points.

The idea is not to see who can uncover the verse first, but who can gain the most points, therefore the teams are to be encouraged to think tactically if they think they know what some of the words might be.

Commentator

1 minute

" Jesus commanded his friends, his disciples, to love one another, just as he had loved them. What does this mean? What was the extent of his love for his friends? "

Verruca pass

 Jesus washes feet (John 13:1–20)

Split the group into teams.
For each team draw a foot on a black/white board and place within them 15 spots. Explain that these spots represent verrucas and the idea is for each team to try to get rid of as many of them as they can to the surrounding teams. This is done by asking each team in turn to pick a number corresponding to one of the questions below. If the team answer correctly, they may give away the appropriate amount of spots to any other team and cross them off their own foot diagram. Each question should be assigned up to four 'give away' spots. The winning team will have the least spots at the end. Each team will need to have Bibles open at John 13:1–20.

Prepare a number of multiple choice questions which are based on John 13:1–17 mixed with general questions about feet, for example:

1 Which of the following are bones on the foot?
 a) Ulna b) mailla c) **tarsal** d) raduis
 (2 give away spots)

2 When Jesus focused on feet what was the festival which they were celebrating at that time?
 a) Christmas b) Easter c) **Passover**
 d) Bar-open-now
 (1 give away spot)

3 What's the name we give to a dog's foot?
 a) hoof b) **paw** c) claw d) flipper
 (3 give away spots)

Commentator 5 minutes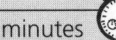

"Jesus gave this commandment after he had done something extraordinary: washing his disciples' feet. This was a common practice in Jesus' day because one's feet would get very sweaty, dirty and dusty as people walked from one place to another. However, the job was reserved for the lowest of the low servant, so why did Jesus do it?

He did it in order to set an example, as he was trying to teach his disciples the importance of servanthood: putting others before yourself, meeting the needs of others first, no matter what they would be, no matter what the cost to yourself. Sacrificial love is what Jesus emphasised. Do we find that in our friendships today?

Love between people was also emphasised by a man in the Bible called Paul. What did he mean when he spoke of loving others?"

Thought:
'Love is…'?

Total Time: up to 16 minutes

The card grab 10 minutes

This game is especially suited to a large room. Make a list of questions based on 1 Corinthians 13:4–8 which each have a different attribute of love as the answer, for example:

1. What is the quality of love which means to be considerate, friendly and helpful? Love is… (kind)
2. What is the quality of love which means not to have too high an opinion of oneself? Love is not… (conceited)

Make a set of cards for each team with a different attribute written on each card. Split into teams and position yourself at the far end of the room. As each question is read out the teams look through their cards and compete to be the first team to hand in the answer. Award points for speed and keep a running score.

Commentator 6 minutes

"Run through the qualities again with your group members, ensuring that they understand every quality and how it can relate to them.

Paul encourages all people to display those qualities. How well do you manage to show these qualities in your friendships?"

Chequered Flag 10 minutes

We all need friends, but how well do you show the qualities that Jesus and Paul encourage their friends to display among themselves so that friendships are strengthened?

This may be quite hard to do by ourselves, but can become easier when we see someone treating us with all the qualities encouraged in the Bible. We can know such a person, because we can know Jesus as our friend, if we ask him. Are we willing to do that?

On the Podium 5 minutes

Award prizes for the following activities: *Friendship outburst, Card quiz, Verruca pass* and *The card grab*.

Lap of Honour 10 minutes

Ask the group members to form pairs and ask them to face each other and imagine themselves looking into a mirror. One person of the pair is to take the lead and the other person is to be their reflection and follow their movements exactly.

Ask them to practise by doing things such as cleaning their teeth, having a wash, combing their hair, squeezing a spot! Make sure both pair members have the chance to lead.

Read to the group Hebrews 13:5b,6. Ask each pair to make up actions which describe/express what is being said in the Bible passage as you read it over and over again. Make sure that each person has the chance of taking the lead. If they want to, allow them to show their creative actions to the rest of the group.

Just like a reflection is always seen in a mirror, so God promises to always be with those who are his friends – what a great God we have!

Close with a prayer of thanks.

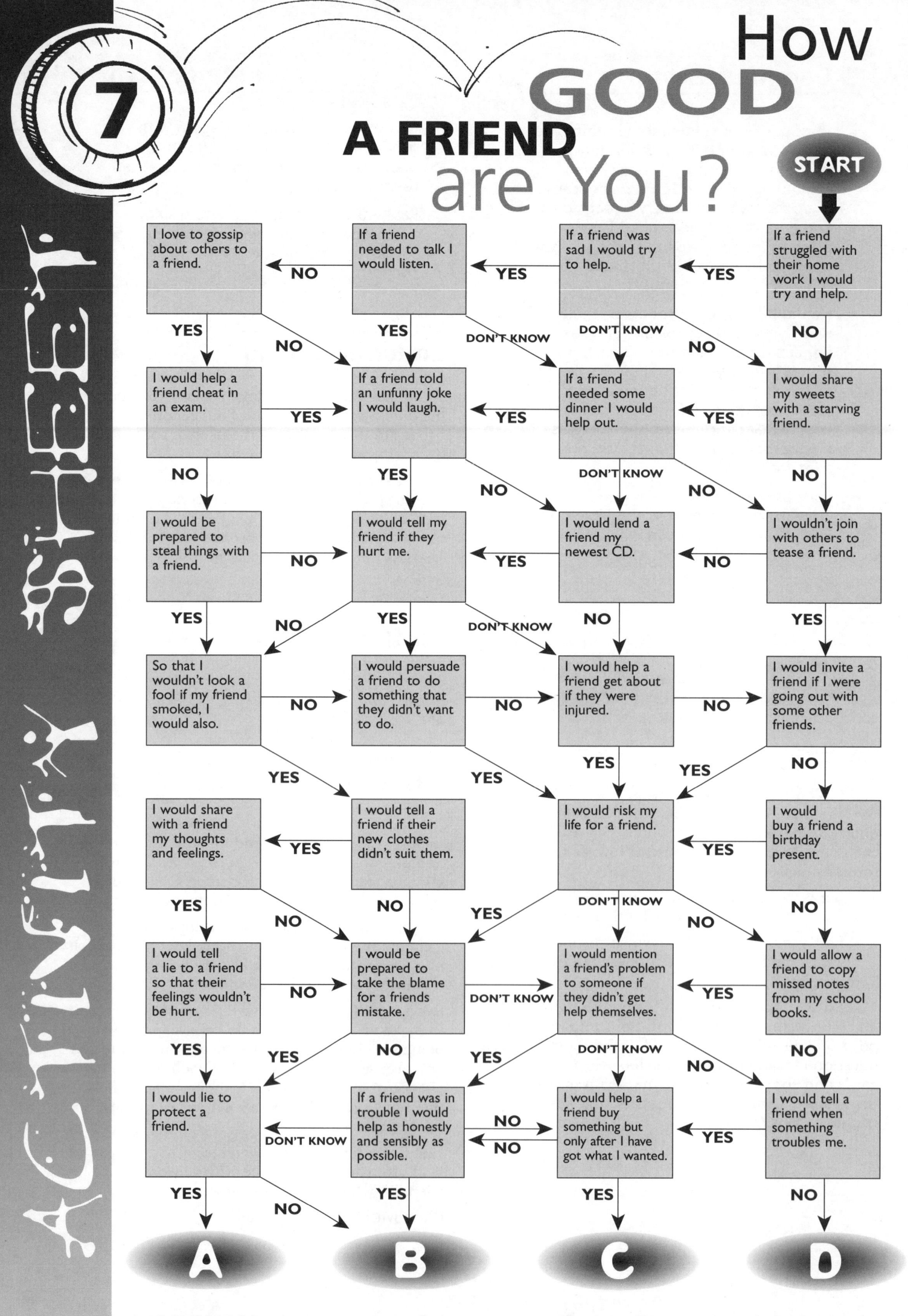

Sex

Qualifying

As young people develop, sex and their sexuality are amongst the bigger issues that they have to face. God knows that this issue affects us all and certainly hasn't kept quiet about it in the Bible. Yet many young people who are not churchgoers believe that God is a spoilsport and anti-sex.

This session seeks to show that God's commands and advice benefit those who are obedient to him. It seeks to uncover what God's views are on sex.

This session isn't meant to explain the physical nature of sex or explore this issue in great depth. What you may find is that the material raises many questions among the young people which they want answering. Therefore it will be more important than ever to be flexible, and to be willing to spread the material over a couple of weeks, in order to deal with their questions.

This session needs to follow on from the previous session on friends.

Starting Grid
(up to 20 minutes)

A Pucker up
up to 10 minutes

Select a number of volunteers. After applying a generous coat of lipstick, ask each volunteer to pucker up and impress a kiss onto a blank sheet of paper. Hold a guessing competition to match up the correct lip print to each volunteer.

B Feel it with your feet
up to 10 minutes

 Bring to the session things that either you use to wrap presents up with and/or gifts which are most commonly given, eg handkerchiefs, money, perfume, bath salts etc.

Depending on the size of your group, either allow them all to participate or ask for several volunteers to come out to the front.

Blindfold the participants and ask them to take off their shoes and, if possible, their socks also. One by one ask them to identify the objects by feeling them with their feet. See who can correctly identify the most.

C Music quiz
10 minutes

 From a recently released pop compilation album play to the group extracts from a selection of about ten songs, which, if possible, have love as the theme. Ask the group to see if they can identify the recording artist(s) and the title of the song, for which they receive one point for each one correctly identified.

Thought:
Following God's commands, instructions and advice is the best course of action that we all can take, no matter what the situation.

Total Time: 27 minutes plus

Decide on either or both of the following activities to explore the miracle of Jesus turning water into wine in John 2. After completing these activities it may be an idea to recap over the story in order to make sure that the group members understand the actual happenings in the Bible incident.

a) Chain letters
up to 10 minutes

 Prepare about 15 sequential multiple choice questions from the passage, like the following examples:

i) Jesus went to a wedding but which town was it in?
   Nazareth, Jerusalem, Cana

ii) Which family member of Jesus was also there?
   Mother, father, brother

Split the group into teams and follow these instructions:

a) Ask one of your prepared questions to the teams. Whichever team answers correctly, wins control of the game.

b) Display the word 'water' on a board. Ask the team in control to add a letter to water to make a word which describes a male server of food. (Answer = Waiter.)

c) If they answer incorrectly, ask another team to give an answer.

If they answer correctly, award the team 10 points and ask another prepared question and so on, using the following clues until water has been successfully turned into wine.

Clue 2: Change a letter in 'waiter' to form a word which is the opposite of blacker. (Answer = whiter.)

Clue 3: Change a letter from 'whiter' to form another 6 letter word, which describes someone who constantly moans. (Answer = whiner.)

Clue 4: Take a letter away and add another one to form a new 6 letter word which describes someone who comes first in a race. (Answer = winner).

Clue 5: Take two letters away to form a new 4 letter word which describes an alcoholic drink. (Answer = wine.)

b) Quiz

upto 15 minutes

Devise a quiz based around the same idea as in the John 8 passage found in the 'Forgiveness' section under the activity entitled 'Forgiven or not?' (see page 86).

When it comes to scoring, have some identical jugs with score marks on them and as the teams score points, fill them up to those marks with water.

Pour their final water total into a measuring jug to give the teams a final score.

Commentator

2 minutes

"In this incident the servants were told by Jesus' mother to listen and obey all the instructions that Jesus gave to them. The problem of no wine was solved and Jesus miraculously changed some water into wine. This demonstrates that as a result of listening and obeying Jesus'/God's commands only good things result. He knows what he's doing and knows what will benefit each one of us the most."

Thought:
Media views on sex

Total Time: 16 minutes

Have I got news for you?

15 minutes

On an OHP/board reveal/write up the following one by one. Split the group into teams. See which team can correctly fill in the gaps of the headlines typically found in young people's magazines. Award 5 points for each correct answer:

1 Our _____ love became real   (stage)
2 Lucious _____ lad   (ad)
3 Get the life, look and _____ you want   (snogs)
4 My holiday _____   (heartbreak)
5 Let's go _____ for boys   (shopping)

Commentator

1 minute

"Relationships are a main feature of young people's magazines. Sex seems to be portrayed with the attitude that if it feels good then do it – but take precautions!! Is this really how God views sex?"

Thought:
God's views on sex

Total Time: 11 minutes

2 become 1

10 minutes

 This game aims to bring to the attention of the young people key Bible verses related to the issue of sex, which will probably bring about many questions. Depending on your group's knowledge of the biblical point of view either choose to answer questions during the game or wait till afterwards when you've covered the biblical aspects pointed out in this game.

Split the group into teams. Each team member will need the use of a Bible – this game will help them find their way around it.

Photocopy onto OHP or make individual activity sheets from page 44. Discover which team can either fill in the missing spaces for one of the questions first or be the one to complete the whole sheet first. Score 5 points for each Bible verse completed first or 10 points for the whole sheet.

Commentator

1 minute

"God created male and female and gave them the gift of sex as a wonderful gift to enrich their lives and love for one another. However this gift was to be enjoyed in the context of a secure, loving relationship which only marriage can provide.

God has a lot to say about people having sexual relationships in other situations."

LAP 3

Thought:
God's views on sex outside of marriage

Total Time: 20 minutes

Bible search — 5 minutes

Display the following Bible references on the OHP/board and see which team can be the quickest in having each member reading the next verse of the given passage in unison from their own Bible.

Award five points for each winning team. The references are: Exodus 20:14; Matthew 19:17; 1 Corinthians 6:12; 1 Corinthians 6:17; Colossians 3:4; 1 Thessalonians 5:28. Ask which verse is the odd one out and award 10 points to the team which gives the correct answer first. (Answer: 1 Thessalonians 5:28, as it has nothing to do with adultery or sexual immorality.)

Commentator — 5 minutes

" These verses talk about adultery and sexual immorality.

Adultery is having sex with someone other than your wife/husband and sexual immorality describes casual sex, ie having sex with a boy/girlfriend. Both practices are always condemned in the Bible as they are an abuse of the gift of sex and marriage that God gives to people.

So why listen to God's advice?

God is motivated by love and always wants the very best for us. The creator of something always makes instructions for the best way to use their creation, as they know that misusing it can harm the user. In the same way God created sex as a wonderful, good gift. He gave instructions to us that the best place to use that gift is in marriage.

What could be the consequences of disobeying God's commandments?

The more dramatic consequences can include such things as having an unwanted child, contracting a disease or experiencing the break-up of the family. Less dramatic consequences, but just as hurtful, can include such things as the sense of being used, guilt and emotional pain.

God wants to save us from all the potential risks and wants us to have a really good, fulfilling sexual relationship which according to him, the maker, can only be truly found in the context of marriage.

Answer any questions that may have arisen from this information. "

Making posters (10 minutes)

Consolidate the teaching by asking them to make advertising posters which sum up God's stance on sex. Ask them to show their work to each other and correct any negative representations of biblical teaching by stressing God's care and concern for each one of us.

Chequered Flag — 10 minutes

The Bible demonstrates time and again that those who choose to listen to and obey God's commands, instructions and guidelines end up with a better deal at the end of the day than those who choose to do their own thing. God created sex and made it very good, but as the Creator he knew that the best time and place for it was within a secure loving relationship such as marriage. This is because he knows that misusing his gift of sex can have far-reaching negative consequences.

If you feel it's appropriate, ask the group members to write on a piece of paper something for which they would like to ask forgiveness from God. Collect them up in a metal bin and if possible set fire to their responses, making sure that it is safe to do so and that there is a fire extinguisher ready nearby. Say a prayer and talk about the nature of God's forgiveness if you need to.

On the Podium — 5 minutes

Award prizes for the following activities: *Feel it with your feet, Music quiz, Chain letters, Quiz, Have I got news for you?* and *2 become 1*.

Lap of Honour — 10 minutes

Read Psalm 119:9–16 which advocates the practice of memorising scripture. As a worshipful act, ask each team to memorise the qualities of love in 1 Corinthians 13:4–8a in whatever way they want to. See which team can memorise the qualities first.

BECOME 2 1

Based on the *Good News Bible*

① Genesis 1:27, 28a

So God created _____ _____, making them to be like himself. He created them _____ and _____, blessed them and said 'Have many _____, so that your descendants will live _____ _____ _____ _____ and bring it under their _____.'

② Genesis 2:24

That is why a man leaves his _____ and _____ and is united with his _____, and they become _____.

③ Genesis 2:25

The man and woman were _____ _____, but they were not _____.

④ Matthew 19:4

_____ answered, 'Haven't you read the _____ that says that in the _____ the _____ made people _____ and _____?' And God said, 'For this reason a man will leave his _____ and _____ and unite with his _____, and the _____ will become one. Man must not _____, the, what God has _____ _____.'

⑤ Ephesians 5:28

Men ought to _____ their _____ just as they love their _____ _____. A man who _____ _____ loves himself.

Loneliness and Rejection

Qualifying

We all experience different moods: sometimes we may feel quite contented, at other times we may feel quite sad and low. In the lives of young people these mood swings can often be like a roller coaster, violently changeable, with the peaks higher and the troughs deeper. During the hard times a young person may be consumed by sad, negative emotions, maybe feeling unloved and lonely. This session seeks to show group members that during the peaks and troughs of life, there is someone to whom we can turn, Jesus, who can give all the love and support that we all need in such times.

Starting Grid

(upto 20 minutes)

A The mood game

Aim: To show that our moods can change many times in a day

Prepare 24 numbered cards with one the following written on each: 1 Alarm; 2 Bathroom; 3 Breakfast; 4 Weather; 5 School bell; 6 Meeting; 7 Assembly; 8 Homework A; 9 Lunch; 10 Exam results; 11 Bullies; 12 Running in the school corridor; 13 School Report; 14 False fire alarm; 15 After school club; 16 Bus; 17 Tea; 18 Homework B; 19 Computer; 20 TV; 21 Music/sport lesson; 22 Youth Club; 23 Plans; 24 Bed.

Split the group into teams. Explain that the idea of the game is to see which team can feel the most positive/happy at the end of a day. Each team starts with a feeling score of 50. Shuffle the cards and on each team's turn, ask members to select a card and throw a dice. Check their dice score roll to find out what happens in each situation and how they feel about it – this is shown through the corresponding feeling score. This score is then added or subtracted from their feeling total. Keep the game moving quickly and play until all or most of the cards are used.

EVENT DETAILS

1) Alarm
1 Fails, so bad tempered —10
2 Fails, so grumpy —6
3 Fails, so irritated —4
4 Goes off, feel OK +1
5 Goes off, feel well-rested +5
6 Goes off, feel ready for anything +10

2) Bathroom
1 Sister in – don't have time to wash —10
2 Toothbrush falls down loo —6
3 Bath overflows —4
4 Normal usage – feel OK +1
5 Feel great after bath +5
6 The bathroom is yours for as long as you like +10

3) Breakfast
1 Nothing in except porridge —10
2 Have to make your own —6
3 Burn your toast —4
4 Have favourite cereal +1
5 Have full cooked breakfast +5
6 Have breakfast in bed +10

4) Weather
1 Raining and have to walk to school —10
2 Foggy and in car so you're late —6
3 Cold and wet —4
4 A grey day +1
5 A sunny day – you feel great +5
6 A heat wave and a soft top car +10

5) School bell
1 School detention —10
2 You were 10 mins late —8
3 You were 5 mins late —4
4 On time +1
5 You were early +5
6 You leave school early +10

6) Meeting
1 Meet a bully and get hurt —10
2 Meet ex-boy/girlfriend —6
3 Meet no one – feel lonely —4
4 Meet friend +1
5 Meet boy/girl you fancy +5
6 Meet boy/girl friend +10

7) Assembly
1 Let's get out of here —10
2 Groan – not you again —6
3 Indifferent —4
4 Quite interesting +1
5 Let's hear more +10

8) Homework A
1 Forgot it – detention —10
2 Forgot – shouted at —8
3 Get 4 lots for tomorrow —4
4 Hand in on time +1
5 Good marks for +5
6 Receive none +10

9) Lunch
1 Only scraps left from canteen —10
2 Forgot butties/food money —8
3 Butties are stale —4
4 Have normal lunch +1
5 Have favourite butty filling +5
6 Treated to lunch by a friend +10

10) Exam results
1 0% —10
2 10% —8
3 30% —4

4 52%	+1	3 Was rubbish	–4	2 Was confiscated	–8
5 75%	+5	4 Was OK	+1	3 Nothing worth watching	–4
6 100%	+10	5 Was good	+5	4 Was OK	+1
11) Bullies		6 Was excellent	+10	5 Had Sky	+5
1 Batter you	–10	**16) School bus home**		6 Was excellent	+10
2 Hit you	–8	1 Didn't turn up	–10	**21) Music/sport lesson**	
3 Tease you	–4	2 Too overcrowded	–8	1 Was rubbish	–10
4 Don't notice you	+1	3 Was late	–4	2 Was boring	–8
5 Get detention	+5	4 Was OK	+1	3 Was not enjoyable	–4
6 Get expelled	+100	5 Was early	+5	4 Was OK	+1
12) Running in the corridor		6 Had a lift instead	+10	5 Was great	+5
1 You're expelled	–10	**17) Tea**		6 Was excellent	+10
2 You get detention	–8	1 Had none	–10	**22) Future**	
3 You get lines	–4	2 Got burnt	–8	1 Visit relatives	–10
4 You get a caution	+1	3 Under cooked	–4	2 Visit dentist	–8
5 You're not caught	+5	4 Microwave meal	+1	3 Go food shopping	–4
6 You never do	+10	5 Had takeaway	+5	4 Please yourself	+1
13) School report		6 Had favourite	+10	5 Go out with friends	+5
1 Complete failure	–10	**18) Homework B**		6 Have a special event	+10
2 No hope	–8	1 Didn't bother with it	–10	**23) Youth club**	
3 Could try harder	–4	2 Couldn't do it	–8	1 Was rubbish	–10
4 OK	+1	3 Was quite hard	–4	2 Was boring	–8
5 Very good	+5	4 Was OK	+1	3 Missed it	–4
6 Excellent	+10	5 Was easy	+5	4 Was OK	+1
14) False fire alarm		6 Had none	+10	5 Was good	+5
1 You get the blame	–10	**19) Your computer**		6 Was excellent	+10
2 You get soaked	–8	1 Broke	–10	**24) Bed**	
3 You get cold	–4	2 Was confiscated	–8	1 Couldn't sleep – worrying	–10
4 A pleasant outing	+1	3 Can't complete a game	–4	2 Couldn't sleep – noise	–8
5 Miss maths	+5	4 Was OK	+1	3 Couldn't sleep – heat	–4
6 Miss a test	+10	5 Attracts popularity	+5	4 Slept OK	+1
15) After school club		6 Have a new game	+10	5 Had good night's sleep	+5
1 Forget about it	–10	**20) Your TV system**		6 Had good night's sleep and lie in	+10
2 Miss lift home	–8	1 Broke	–10		

Commentator

1 minute

"From day to day we will experience many different situations which can, in turn, affect our emotions and moods. One moment we can be extremely happy, the next we can be very irritated. Coping with this roller-coaster ride of emotions can often be quite hard."

LAP 1

Thought:
People in the Bible experienced hard times and rejection

Total Time: 25 minutes

Tax collectors game

Up to 20 minutes

Aim: To stimulate the bad feeling there was towards tax collectors in biblical times. (Be careful though not to let such feeling get out of hand.)

Photocopy and enlarge the game board and cards on page 48. Split your group into five teams and give each team an occupation. Explain that they are all living in Israel and in order to make a living they need to roll the dice and move around the game board collecting materials/ingredients for their job. Apart from the tax collectors, each team starts with 100 Denarii with which to buy their materials. They may also exchange saleable goods for money if they are in the market place.

The tax collectors patrol the streets of the town to collect taxes for the Romans and make a living for themselves. Taxes may be collected when the tax collectors land on the same square as another team, or if a team lands on one of the shaded squares representing a permanently manned tax booth. Taxes may not be collected in shops or houses. Tax collectors have the advantage of moving twice the number on the dice.

The amount of tax due is calculated by another roll

of the dice: score 1 or 2 equals 3 Denarii; 3 or 4 equals 10 Denarii; 5 or 6 equals 20 Denarii. If any team cannot pay their taxes, they miss one turn.

Play until the game has produced the desired effect.

Commentator   5 minutes

"Ask the group members how they feel towards the tax collector's team, and why they feel those emotions. Ask the group members what they would do to them if they lived in such an environment.

Fill in some background information on the lifestyle and social position of tax collectors in the New Testament.

I'm sure that despite their wealth they would have been sad, lonely and isolated people."

Thought:
Jesus reaches out to the 'unloved'
Total Time: up to 30 minutes

Split the group into teams and give one of the following Bible passages to each of the teams to read (if you have previously used Lap 1, make sure the stories follow on): Luke 19:1–10 (Jesus and Zacchaeus); Mark 1:40–45 (Jesus healing a person suffering from leprosy).

Video/radio diaries   28 minutes

Video diaries have recently been very popular on television. Ask each team to put themselves in either Zacchaeus' or the healed man's shoes and then ask them to record, using a camcorder or a cassette recorder, their feelings throughout the 'day'. Some suggestions for Zacchaeus are:
• How he felt that morning before he met Jesus;
• How he felt when up the tree waiting;
• How he felt when taking Jesus back to his house;
• How he felt when preparing a meal for Jesus
• How he felt once Jesus had gone.

For each scene, each team could take it in turns being the principal character or elect only one team member to play the principal character throughout. (If using cassette recorder, provide materials which can be used for sound effects.)

Give them 10 minutes to prepare, then 10 minutes to film or record the scenes. Show the finished results to everyone.

Commentator   2 minutes

"Read out Matthew 11:28–30. Just as Jesus shared the pain of Zacchaeus/the man with leprosy, in this Bible passage he invites us to share the hard times that we all experience with him. How do we do this? By talking to him, just like you may talk to a friend. This is called prayer."

Chequered Flag   5 minutes

Throughout our life there will be times when we feel hurt, lonely and rejected. Throughout his life Jesus confronted and helped people who experienced similar emotions. He made promises to his followers that he would always be there for them and help them through those times – and those promises still apply today!

On the Podium   2 minutes

Award prizes for the following activities: *The mood game* and *The tax collectors game*.

Lap of Honour   8 minutes

Pass the Bomb

Give all members an envelope, paper and a pen. On the paper ask them to write something that they would like to share with Jesus. Put this in the envelope and ask them to seal it. On the outside of the envelope ask them to write a 'thank you' prayer.

Split the group into four teams, and play 'Pass the bomb'. The aim of the game is to get rid of as many envelopes as possible. This is done by sending two people at a time to another team's area and giving them an envelope. The receiving team must accept the envelope. Only when a runner returns can a team send someone else out. See how many envelopes they can get rid of in a minute, and add up the score at the end. Use this as a symbolic way of giving their thoughts and feelings to God. Read out Philippians 4:6,7.

COOK	CLOTHES MAKER	CARPENTER	POTTER
Cake 15d	Coat 15d	Table 15d	Water Holder 15d
Bread 5d	Head Dress 5d	Chair 10d	Pot 10d
Bread 5d	Socks 5d	Chair 10d	Plate 10d
Cake 10d	Shoes 10s	Toy 5d	Cup 5d
Cake 10d	Shoes 10d	Toy 5d	Pot 5d

COOK'S EXCHANGES	CLOTHES MAKER'S EXCHANGES	CARPENTER'S EXCHANGES	POTTER'S EXCHANGES
Flour – 5d from the merchant	**Needle** – 5d from Mr Metal	**Axe** – 5d from Mrs Brakett	**Clay** – 5d from the clay works
Water 0 from the collection point	**Fleece** – 10d from the animal market	**Chisel** – 5d from the overseas company	**Wood for kiln** – 10d from the forest
Yeast – 5d from Mrs Booth	**Animal Hyde** – 5d from the cooks house	**Metal nails** – 5d from Mr Metal	**Clay mould** – 5d from the carpenters
Lamb – 15d frmo the animal market	**Linen** – 5d from the overseas company	**Hammer** – 10d from the potter	**Paint** – 10d from the clothes maker
Wood from the fire – 10d from the wood	**A loom** – 10d from the carpenter	**Wood** – 10d from the forest	**Wire** – 5d from Mrs Brackett
Collect 15d from the carpenters	Collect 15d from the potter	Collect 15d from the clothes maker	Collect 5d from the cook
Total savings 100d	**Total savings 100d**	**Total savings 100d**	**Total savings 100d**

GAMEBOARD
TAX COLLECTORS GAME

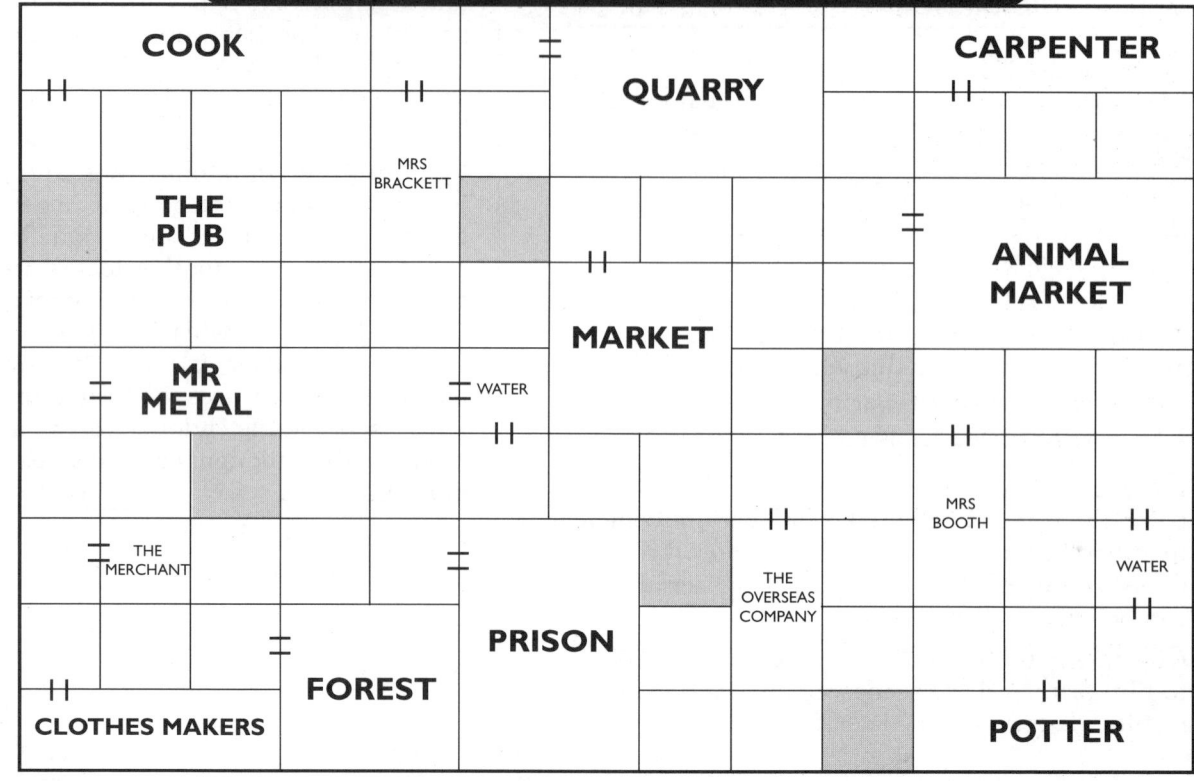

Jealousy

Qualifying

This session seeks to help the group members understand the times when they feel jealous. It seeks to show what jealousy can lead to and to demonstrate that true fulfilment in life comes only when we include Jesus in our lives.

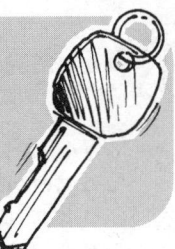

Starting Grid
(up to 25 minutes)

Aim: To show that comparing abilities is often the cause of jealousy

A They've gotta... and I want one!

up to 10 minutes

This is a slight variation of a well-known memory game. Form the group into a circle. Ask someone to start and to tell the group their name and something about a possession of theirs of which they are really proud. The person next to them also tells the group their name and a possession they're proud of, then reminds the group of the previous person's name and possession, declaring 'I want one too'. The third person tells the group their name and a possession they're proud of, and reminds the group of the previous two names and possessions, declaring 'I want all of these'. Continue around the circle until the last person has to try and remember everyone's name and possession.

B Sports master

25 minutes

This is ideally suited to a large hall and to a group who are active, but not necessarily all into sport. Before the group arrives, set up different activities around the hall. Split the group into pairs and give them a list of activities and a pencil to record their score. Explain that each person will have 1.5 minutes to discover what score they can obtain at each activity. Activities may include:

- How many words can you make from a long word?
- How many squat thrusts, star jumps, sit ups etc can you do?
- How many points can you score, throwing something at a target?
- How many times can you run from one side of the hall to another?
- How many times can you continually bounce a ball with a table tennis racket?
- How many times can you continually bounce a shuttlecock with a racket?

Use a whistle to start and stop them. Keep the game moving and allow 30 seconds for change between the activities. Collect their score sheets and announce their scores at the end.

Use this activity to point out how we all compare ourselves with others, and how it's easy to become jealous of those who are successful.

Thought:
Ways in which group members experience jealousy

Total Time: 32 minutes

Jealous of what?

up to 30 minutes

Split the group into small teams consisting of 3 to 5 members, depending on which of the following activities you decide to do.

Prepare either cards with the following examples on or make a spinning arrow on a pie chart, with the examples labelled on it. Examples: achievements, bag, bike, computer, exams, family, house, jeans, job, looks, personality, pets, pocket money, popularity amongst friends, relationships with opposite sex, sports jacket, talents and trainers.

For each team either spin the arrow ten times to see what categories they get or shuffle the cards and ask them to pick ten at random.

Each team is to look at their topics and in each case decide which are the best type of these topics to have, items which normally would make themselves or their friends jealous if they saw someone else with them.

Obtain as many catalogues and general magazines as possible and give to each team scissors, paste, pens and a large sheet of paper. Ask them to draw an outline of a person on the paper and look through the magazines so that they can cut out and stick on images which express their ideas.

When it's time to finish the activity, ask everyone to present their creations.

Commentator

2 minutes

"We can all experience jealousy in many different ways as we compare ourselves and our possessions with others. Some may not see jealousy as a problem or a serious issue, but jealousy can be harmful. It can become such a powerful emotion in someone's life that they can go to extremes in order to satisfy their desires."

Thought:
Jealousy can give rise to many harmful effects

Total Time: 25 minutes

Pick 'em

23 minutes

Split the group into two teams.
Choose two volunteers who are good at the game 'Charades' or 'Pictionary'. These volunteers will not belong to any team and therefore are classed as your helpers. In turn give your helpers the following descriptions of biblical events and ask them to either act them out, draw the scene on a board or do both. Give the volunteers a maximum of a minute to act/draw the incident. (Be careful not to allow this activity to drag.) Move on to the next Bible incident when each one has been guessed.

1) Joseph's brothers (Genesis 37)
Joseph's father Jacob loved Joseph more than all his other brothers, and to show his love for him he made a richly ornamented robe to wear. This angered his brothers. Joseph also had many dreams, many of which seemed to imply that one day all his family would bow down before him. His brothers grew more and more jealous of him and decided one day to kill him.

2) Saul's jealousy of David (1 Samuel 18: 6-16)
After David had killed the giant Goliath with his sling and stones, David accompanied his king, Saul, back home. All the women came to greet them, singing, dancing and playing musical instruments. They sang, 'Saul has killed thousands but David has killed tens of thousands.' Saul became so jealous of David that he tried to kill David by throwing his spear at him, twice!

3) Squabbling disciples (Mark 9:35)
One day Jesus' disciples were arguing as to which among them was the greatest. Jesus told them straight that if anyone wants to be first, they must be the last, and the servant of them all.

4) The jealous Jewish authorities (Acts 5:17-42)
After Jesus had died and rose again, his disciples were given power to do miracles by the Holy Spirit. The religious leaders saw the popularity of the disciples and grew so jealous that they had the disciples thrown into prison. They wanted to kill them. God foiled their plans by sending an angel to release them.

5) The lost son's brother (Luke 15)
In Jesus' famous parable, when a father's youngest son returned home after wasting his inheritance money, the father was so pleased to see him that he threw a great party. The eldest son refused to attend because despite his faithfulness, he had never been rewarded in such a way.

Commentator

2 minutes

"Jealousy often spills over into anger and violence, showing that jealousy is a very powerful emotion. If it isn't recognised and dealt with in its early stages, than it can give rise to many harmful effects. So how does God want us to live?"

Thought:
Having a correct perception about ourselves

Total Time: 27 minutes

Chance it!

25 minutes

Before the session think about the talents, gifts and interests present in the young people in your group and devise up to 10 tasks for them to do, which will use their different gifts and abilities. Write some questions based on 1 Corinthians 12 for the teams to answer.

Split the group into teams. For each team draw ten empty boxes in a row on a board. On your master copy decide where to place three hot spots and your devised tasks, as in the example on the activity sheet (see page 52).

Photocopy, distribute and read to the group 1 Corthinians 12.

Determine which team will go first by discovering which team throws the highest dice score.

Round 1

On each team's turn, they are to decide how many questions from the Bible passage they want to answer (1, 2 or 3 questions), as these will determine how many moves they can make. If they get all the questions correct, they can move onto round 2. If they answer incorrectly, the questions are passed to the next team in turn. Whichever team answers the questions correctly, moves on to round 2.

Round 2

If a team answers three questions correctly, they are entitled to move three places along the board. Give them the first task which they need to attempt and allow them a maximum of 30 seconds in which to complete it. If the team achieves the task in the given time, they can either choose to stick on that square or move on to the next task and so on, until they have moved their three places. If they fail to complete a task or if they hit a hotspot, they move back to the square they were on before and the next team has their turn.

The winning team is the first to reach square 10.

Commentator 2 minutes

" Explain that in the game each team needed to work together in order to successfully achieve the given tasks. Some people excelled at some tasks but may have had difficulty with others. However in order for the team to be successful, everyone had to work together so that their strengths and weaknesses complemented each other.

The Bible passage emphasised the fact that we are all different and are given different gifts by God. Instead of continually comparing ourselves with others and becoming jealous, God wants us to realise and be thankful for the gifts and resources that we have been given.

If you have time, use the parable of the talents (Matthew 25:14-30) in order to emphasis the point. Point out that the two faithful servants were rewarded more because they were faithful with the little they had been given. "

Chequered Flag 3 minutes

When we feel jealous of another person, let's remember that it's such a strong emotion that if we let it get out of hand, it may lead us to do something that we may come to regret. Instead of focusing on what others have and what we may be lacking, let's adopt the view that God wants us to have. Remember that God values us all the same, as individual precious human beings. Be thankful for the gifts that God has given us and try to use them to serve him, because we all have an equally important role to play. Don't forget that those who are faithful in small matters will be given more.

Knowing that we are all precious to God and are accountable to him for all that he gives to us, can free us from making comparisons with others, which can potentially cause us much heartache.

On the Podium 2 minutes

Award prizes for the following activities: *Sports Master*, *I want to...*, *Pick 'em* and *Chance it!*.

Lap of Honour 20 minutes

Thank you for this food

Buy lots of chocolate bars for the group members to devour and label them with qualities that God promises to give to his children eg, love, security, peace, help etc. Once everyone has had their fill, read Isaiah 53:1 and 2 and reaffirm that in Christ we can become whole, complete and satisfied. Compare their empty wrappers to the fact that even though everyone might be satisfied now, the satisfaction is only a temporary feeling.

Finish by allowing every member to thank God for his goodness in their hearts. The worship song 'Is anyone thirsty?' would be an appropriate song to play at this point.

CHANCE it

ACTIVITY SHEET 10

1	Name 3 members of Man Utd Football team.
2	Eat at least 2 apple pies in the given time.
3	Do 10 press ups.
4	**HOT SPOT**
5	This passage refers to the body. Draw a picture of an eye.
6	What's the answer to this? 2x3x9x0=
7	**HOT SPOT**
8	Play a tune on a kazoo and someone else dance to it.
9	**HOT SPOT**
10	Can you guess the price of this item of clothing in the given time?

Lying

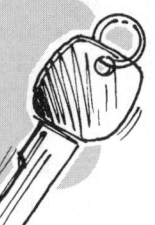

Qualifying

Lying can be an instinctive defensive reaction in the best of us, even to some characters we find in the Bible. This session seeks to highlight the problem we all can have with lying and compares our behaviour with that of Jesus. Our imperfect state is no excuse for lying.

Starting Grid
(up to 20 minutes)

A Mr and Miss Smoothy    8 minutes

Choose several volunteers who like talking to do this activity. Ask them to think of a subject about which they could talk for 45 seconds. Give them a piece of paper and ask them to write down up to five lies which they should try and include in their short talk.

The other group members listen to each speaker in turn and try and determine the lies they include. Award a prize to the speaker who had the most undetected lies.

B Call my bluff    20 minutes

Before the game write out on separate cards definitions of the following words: deceive, dissimulate and guile. Then invent and write out two false definitions for each word. On each card include the words 'true' or 'false' as appropriate.

Split into two teams. The idea is that three members of one team each read out a definition of a word and the opposing team has to guess which is correct. If they guess correctly, award them a point; if not, the bluffing team gain a point. The roles are then reversed for the next word, and so on until all of the words have been used.

C Blindfold walk    10 minutes

Aim: To show that anyone can lie, even those we trust!

Design and prepare an obstacle course in your meeting room. Choose two people to be blindfolded and place them at one end of the course. Choose another two people to stand by each blindfolded member and give one of them a baton. Whoever holds this baton will tell the blindfolded member wrong directions; whoever isn't holding the baton will call out correct directions, in order for them to complete the course.

Explain to those blindfolded that it is a race to see which of them can first reach the end of the course. In order to do that they are to listen to the instructions of the two non-blindfolded members next to them, one of whom is going to lie about the correct directions and the other is going to tell the truth. Halfway through the game, get the two people giving directions to swap the baton, thus reversing their roles. See what effect this has! (Please keep safety in mind while playing this game.)

D Up the garden path    10 minutes

When group members arrive, ask them to go and see someone urgently (create a suitable reason). Have that person send them somewhere else and so forth. See how long it takes for group members to realise they are being taken for a ride!

Commentator
1 minute

"In today's session we are examining somthing that we have all had experience of: lying. We all lie from time to time, but we're not alone – even some characters in the Bible lie. But why do we do it?"

Thought:
All people can lie for different reasons, including those found in the Bible!

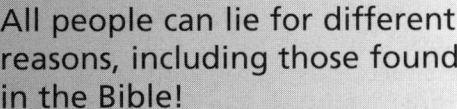

Total Time: 20 minutes

The big pork pie    15 minutes

Split the group into teams. Draw a lie detector score chart (use your imagination) on a board for each team. Explain to each team that they are a particular character from the Bible and that they are required to answer ten questions related to their life.

Ask a team their questions (see below for an example). For every incorrect answer, increase your lie detector gauge by one. The team who told the least lies (eg, got the most answers correct) is the winner.

Use the following questions for Peter as a guide. If you need further characters then devise questions for Joseph's brothers (Genesis 37), Ananias and Sapphira (Acts 5:1–11) or Cain (Genesis 4:1–16).

Peter
1. Do you like fish? (Yes, because he was a fisherman.)
2. I believe you knew Jesus for more than 5 years is this correct? (No, only about 3 years.)
3. How would you describe your friendship with Jesus: casual, good or very good? (Very good.)
4. You were part of Jesus followers called disciples weren't you? (Yes.)
5. It was John your other friend who first described Jesus as the Messiah wasn't it? (No, see Luke 9:20.)
6. Were you with Jesus when he revealed his true nature as the Son of God? (Yes, see Luke 9:28–36.)
7. Didn't you say that you were ready to go to prison with Jesus? (Yes, see Luke 22:33)
8. Didn't you say that you were ready to die with Jesus? (Yes, see Luke 22:33.)
9. Do you, Peter, strike out at people using a sword? (Yes, see John 18:10.)
10. Despite knowing Jesus closely for three years, being his best friend, being the first to declare that he was the Messiah, didn't you declare three times that you didn't know him? (Yes, see Luke 22:54–62.)

Commentator
5 minutes

"Why did these Bible characters lie? Are their reactions similar to ours? In what way? The Bible is very honest about the people who are within its pages as it clearly shows their strengths and weaknesses. Sometimes we may view Bible characters as 'super spiritual' or 'super holy'. However, we read that they were human just like us and therefore it should come as no surprise that they sometimes made the same mistakes that we do. Perhaps they lied for the same reason that we sometimes do, eg to save face, to avoid trouble, to avoid the consequences of our actions etc. So does lying matter?"

Thought:
Jesus' example shows us that he never told lies but always told the truth, because he was the Truth.

Total Time: 22 minutes

Jesus told the truth
8 minutes

Enlarge the activity sheet on page 56 entitled 'Jesus the Truth' and place it on a board in front of the group members. Write each of the Bible references contained within it on separate cards and place them also on a board.

Split the group into teams. Give each team an NIV Bible and allocate them a colour. On your word a member of each team goes to the front, picks up a Bible reference card and takes it back to their team to find that Bible reference as quickly as possible. Once they have found it, they all stand up and read it out loudly.

Acknowledge the winning team by colouring in (on the 'Jesus the truth' sheet) the Bible verse they have just read out in their team colour. The teams then go to the front to get another Bible reference card. Continue until all the references have been found. The team who has found and read the most Bible verses wins.

Commentator
2 minutes

"When Jesus used the phrase 'I tell you the truth', he wanted to emphasise the particular point of truth that he was making, and as you can see from the amount of times he said that phrase, he had many important things to say. That phrase also gives us a clue as to the example that Jesus set us on earth: he never lied but always told the truth. Why?"

Add a line — 7 minutes

Duplicate and enlarge the following. Discover who can be first to complete the claim of Jesus found in John 14:6, by adding one line to form each correct letter.

I AM THE WAY,
THE TRUTH
AND THE LIFE
NO ONE COMES TO
THE FATHER
EXCEPT BY ME

Commentator — 5 minutes

"Read Matthew 15:18–20. Jesus knew that when we lie, no matter how big or small the lies, they hurt us and other people. Lying matters to God, because he cares about us and doesn't want us to damage ourselves or any friendship that we may have with him. So then how does God want us to live?

The Bible encourages us all to have a friendship with Jesus. Those who have such a friendship are said to walk in the light. The Bible encourages us to live in a way that pleases Jesus following his example. However, despite our best efforts, sometimes we will be just like those Bible characters who let God down by lying. The Bible says when this happens we need to realise our mistakes, say sorry to God, ask for his forgiveness and start afresh trying to live the way Jesus would like us live like (John 15:5)."

Chequered Flag — 5 minutes

It is good to know that not only do we make mistakes by lying sometimes, but that people in the Bible also made mistakes and lied. This doesn't excuse our mistakes because when we compare our lives with the example and words of Jesus we realise that he thinks lying is a very serious matter because it hurts us and our relationship with God. He set us an example of being truthful in every situation, backing up his claim of being the Truth. We are therefore encouraged to have a friendship with Jesus and follow his example, knowing that if we do make a mistake and lie, we can ask God to forgive us and help us to start afresh. In doing so we are said to live in the light rather than the dark.

On the Podium — 5 minutes

Award prizes for the following activities: *Mr and Miss Smoothy*, *Call my bluff*, *Blindfold walk*, *The big pork pie*, *Jesus told the truth* and *Add a line*.

Lap of Honour — 6 minutes

Light and dark

If possible, darken the room and then light a candle. Ask the group members to shout out words which describe the qualities of the light and make a note of them. Blow out the candle and ask them to do the same for darkness.

Relight the candle again and read John 1:1–5. Relate the qualities of light described by the group members to God in a prayer of thanksgiving and then pray for help for each of the group members as they seek to follow Jesus' example.

Jesus the Truth

ACTIVITY SHEET

- Matthew 18:3
- Matthew 17:20
- Matthew 16:28
- Matthew 13:17
- Matthew 11:11
- Matthew 10:23
- Matthew 10:42
- Matthew 10:15
- Matthew 8:10
- Matthew 6:2
- Matthew 6:16
- Matthew 6:5
- Matthew 5:18
- Matthew 5:26

Anger

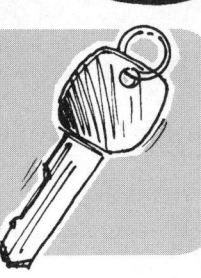

Qualifying

Anger is a very powerful emotion we all experience and handle in different ways. This session seeks to assure group members that anger is a normal human response to certain situations, but also to show that the consequences of anger can either be positive or negative.

Starting Grid
(up to 16 minutes)

Ⓐ Observation quiz
8 minutes

Split the group into teams and show a video clip of people becoming angry with each other, using a film or TV soap. Ask observation questions to discover which team was the most observant.

Ⓑ Shouting contest
8 minutes

Choose some volunteers and give each a short article from a newspaper. They are to stand in front of the other group members and shout them out, in turn, as angrily and as loudly as possible. The listening group members are to put their fingers in their ears while each volunteer shouts their article. They then decide which volunteer was the angriest and loudest.

Ⓒ Slow motion anger
8 minutes

The following two activities show how anger can lead to violence:

i) Toy scramble (8 minutes)

Clear the centre of the room and ask the group members to stand in the space provided. Explain that you want them to imagine they are all Christmas shoppers trying to find a toy which is the latest craze. It's Christmas Eve and every shop has sold out of them.

Place two toys in the centre of the room. Explain that they are all in a toy shop when a shout goes up as someone sees two of these toys. As a result there is a mad scramble for them.

Ask the group to act out the resulting scene in slow motion, which will be full of anger and maybe violence. Explain that no physical contact is allowed and that everyone is to enter into this play-acting in good humour. Watch or video the scene of mayhem that ensues.

Ⓓ Anger commentary
8 minutes

Ask the group to name situations which make people angry. Choose two volunteers to stand at the front and mime in slow motion one such event, plus two people to do a comical running commentary on the mime. Allow time for several of these sketches.

Thought:
What makes you angry? How do you react?

Total Time: 21 minutes

Anger vote
10 minutes

Give each member two pieces of paper and a pen. Ask them to write on each piece something that makes them really angry. Put the papers in a box at the front of the room.

Read out the slips of paper. Each group member is to listen, think how they would react and vote accordingly by:

- Folding their arms, if they would not be affected by the situation.
- Pointing a finger in the air, if they would mildly be affected.
- Punching a fist in the air, if they would explode into an uncontrollable rage.

Keep a tally of their responses and at the end announce the results, indicating which things create the most anger within the group.

Commentator
1 minute

"Many different things can make us angry, but how do we express the anger that we feel?"

Stoke the boiler
8 minutes

Give everyone a copy of the activity sheet on page 60 and ask them to complete it.

Commentator
2 minutes

"Discuss how the group members react in each case and what the consequences can be for reacting in this way.

As an introduction to the next lap, discuss with the group whether they feel that anger is ever justified and in what cirmcumstances."

LAP 2 — Thought:
Comparing the anger of Jesus to that of the religious authorities who stoned Stephen.

Total Time: up to 22 minutes

It is important to compare the following incidents of anger.

Temple re-enactment
5 minutes

Split the group into teams and read John 2:13–17. Each team is to make a supply of projectiles from material provided, eg newspapers, socks etc. In a corner of the room set up a target area by using unwanted household items such as plastic bottles and cans etc. Label these objects as sheep, cattle, coins and money changers. In turn, each team throws their projectiles at the objects to see how many they can knock down.

Commentator
3 minutes

"In this passage we read about Jesus becoming angry over the situation of the Jewish temple in Jerusalem. In that place there were people who were exploiting those who had come a long way to worship God. They were unfairly making money out of the faithful believers. Jesus knew this was wrong and that the practices displeased his Father. This is an example of justifiable and positive anger, as it was motivated by a love and concern of others rather than a selfish desire."

Stephen, the first martyr
12 minutes

Explain that you are going to focus attention on a man called Stephen.

Jigsaw assembly

Draw a figure on a piece of A4 paper and write the following qualities on it: he was a servant (Acts 6:5); he had great faith (Acts 6:5); he was full of the Holy Spirit; he was richly blessed by God (Acts 6:8) and he had power to do miraculous signs (Acts 6:8). Photocopy the piece of paper and cut each one up to produce a jigsaw, enough for one per team. Devise about twenty questions on the subject of Stephen.

Ask the teams a question, who are to write their answer down. Ask each team to declare their answer. Those with the correct answer receive a part of their jigsaw. The first team to get all twenty pieces wins.

Explain that Stephen was appointed by the disciples to look over the distribution of food to ensure that everyone had an equal share. Yet he was more than a servant as he had many gifts from God, and wasn't scared to share his faith with others. This caused him to became noticed by the Jews who took a dislike to him and argued with him (Acts 7:9) However, God gave Stephen such wisdom that they couldn't win any of the arguments (Acts 7:10). The Jews then started a smear campaign and got some people to spread rumours about Stephen and what he had been saying (Acts 7:11). These rumours were believed and so he was arrested and asked to answer for the reports that people had been hearing about him (Acts 7:12). Some of the Jews weren't prepared to listen to him and believe all he had to say. In fact, they became so angry with the things that he was saying that they dragged him out of the city to stone him to death (Acts 7:57,58).

Stone Stephen

Place small targets all over the body of a leader. Members of each team take it turns to throw soft projectiles at the leader, trying to hit the targets, for each of which they score one point. Add up the team's collective score and discover who has won. To make this activity more interesting, ask the leader to move about or to even get chased by their pursuer.

Commentator
2 minutes

"The Jews who listened to Stephen experienced anger (Acts 7:54). Their anger was not motivated by love and concern for others but by an arrogant, conceited and selfish attitude which said that they were right and everyone else was wrong. This led the Jews to kill Stephen (Acts 7:60) – not a very godly action for such supposedly godly people!

Anger can be both a positive and negative quality, depending on our motivation. So how can we control our anger so that we avoid its negative consequences?"

LAP 3 — Thought:
How to control a hasty temper

Total Time: 22 minutes

Cool it
12 minutes

Present the group with a number of scenarios in which someone is likely to become angry or lose their temper. For example:

1. Someone has pushed in front of you in a queue when you have already been waiting for ages.
2. You have been looking forward to your friend's party but now your parents expect you to babysit your little sister.
3. Your ex-friend has told tales about you.
4. You've been grounded for smoking.

Ask each team to decide how they would probably react. Share these ideas then read James 3:2–8. Ask the group to decide if their reaction would be likely to make things better or start a fiery argument. What would be the probable outcome? In the light of the Bible verse, can they suggest a better course of action?

Commentator
2 minutes

"Consolidate the point by discovering who will be the first to solve the following Bible verse puzzle (James 1:19):

Rmmbr ths my dr brthrs! vryn mst b qck t lstn, bt slw t spk nd slw t bcme ngry. Mn's ngr ds nt chv Gd's rghts prps.

(For the answer, just add vowels.)"

Chequered Flag
5 minutes

We can all experience anger. Sometimes anger can be good, if motivated by love and concern for others. This was seen through the example of Jesus who, as a result of his concern for others, got angry and put an end to the exploitation of Jewish worshippers. However, anger can also be very negative as it can lead to tragic consequences, as in the case of Stephen. As anger is a very powerful emotion, the Bible encourages us to keep it under control.

What are we going to do the next time we experience anger?

Finish by reading Ephesians 4:26,27.

On the Podium
5 minutes

Award prizes for the following activities: Observation quiz, Shouting contest, Temple re-enactment and Stephen the first martyr (Jigsaw and Stone Stephen).

Lap of Honour
8 minutes

High 5

Read Hebrews 4:14–16

Explain that Jesus knows what it's like to be human and what it's like to experience anger, but chose to please his Father rather than himself. This is a great source of encouragement to all of us because if we struggle with anger and share our feelings with him, then he can and will help us. This deserves a response from us.

Ask every member to draw around a hand, on paper, then cut out the resulting shape. Ask them to respond to God's willingness to help us by writing a prayer of thanks or petition on these hands. Stick them on a wall and with a prayer.

Stoke the Boiler

ACTIVITY SHEET

Show how you react when in these states of anger by drawing in the faces at each stage

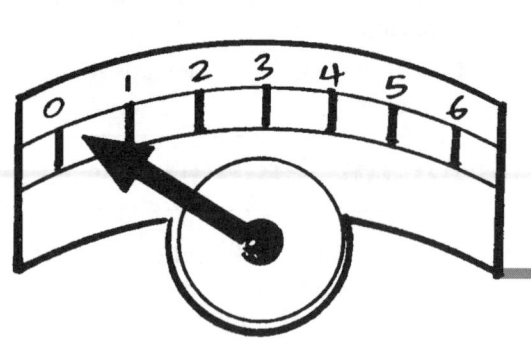 Bothered

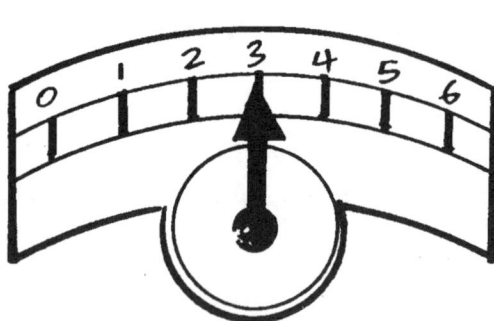 Irritated

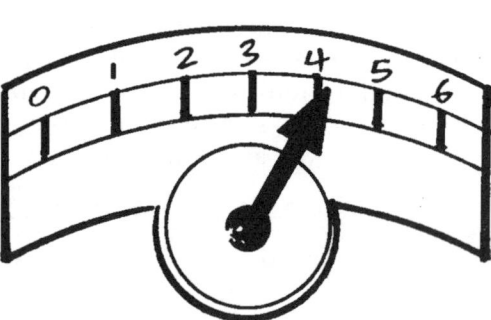 Fuming

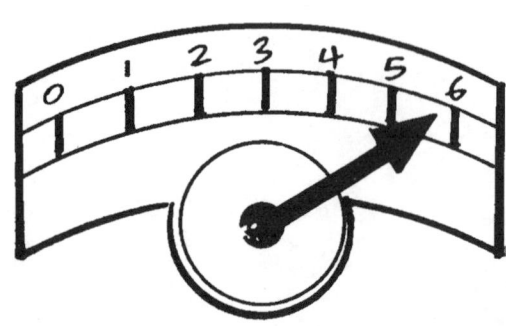 About to Blow!!

Death and the after life

Qualifying

Death is one thing we can all be sure that we are going to experience, and as such is often a taboo subject. This session seeks to allay fears and stress the wonderful promise Christ gives of eternal life.

While many of the activities are quite light-hearted, please be aware of individual members of your group and whether or not they have had experience of bereavement recently. Some activities may not be appropriate if this is the case.

Starting Grid
(10 minutes minimum)

A Dead or alive — 10 minutes

Prepare a list of up to twenty names of famous people. Include a mixture of people from the areas of film, TV, politics, music, sport, world affairs etc. Approximately half should be people who have died. Jesus Christ should be the last person on the list.

Split the group into teams. Each team has to decide whether the person is dead or alive.

Award points for each correct answer.

B Deadly handshake — 5 minutes

Buy three different makes of sweets such as mints. In the group discreetly distribute some of each type amongst the group. Explain that everyone should go around the group shaking hands with each other for about two minutes. The people with mints in their hands are to pass them on to the person who shakes hands with them. Explain that the idea of the game is to get rid of any mints obtained as quickly as possible, by shaking other people's hands. Stress that one cannot refuse to take a mint.

Once the time is over, find out who has the mints and then explain the significance of each mint. For example,

- Those with mint A are going on holiday and have to have an injection but will have a great time.
- Those with mint B have a cold, which may mean a few days in bed but soon will be better.
- Those with mint C have contracted a rare laughing disease and unfortunately just died!

C Make a coffin — 10 minutes

Warning: Be careful where you use this activity. I guarantee young people love it!

Split the group into teams. Provide an amount of cardboard and newspaper for each team.

Explain that one member of their team tragically has died and that it is up to the rest of the team to provide the best send off possible.

Task 1

Each team needs to sort out who the casualty is and then use the materials provided to build a coffin around the 'dead' person. They do not need to build a lid as once they have formed the sides they are to lay their 'body' out in the most dignified and realistic way as possible (even provide some flour for the body, if appropriate). Let each team use their imaginations, but if need be suggest that flowers on the 'body' would look nice.

Task 2

Explain that when judged, each team will be also be marked on the quality of the mourning for their fellow team member.

Judge each team and award points for each entry.

Commentator — 1 minute

"If there is one thing we can be sure of it's this: one day we will experience death – not only the death of a person known to us, but also our own death. It's not surprising that this is not a popular subject to talk about! Yet what may seem such a negative subject, springs to life with hope and promise when Jesus gets involved."

LAP 1

Thought:
We're in good company if we fear death

Total Time: 17 minutes

Help, the boat's sinking!
15 minutes

Split the group into teams. Read Mark 4:35–41. Each team will require a simple diagram of a sailing boat which has been marked off into approximately ten segments. Stick these up where everyone can see them. Ask a question. The first to put up their hand and answer wins control of the game.

That team throws a dice and uses the number rolled to decide how many segments to colour in on the other teams' boats (these signify damage). The number is allowed to be split between teams. The winning team is the one with the least boat segments coloured in. Award points depending on their success.

Questions should include both factual details of the story and more imaginative responses, for example: 'What time of day was it?'; 'The best team to do an impression of someone just waking up' and 'Mime how you think the disciples felt at the end of the situation'.

Commentator
2 minutes

" If we are fearful of death, then we are in good company, because even Jesus' disciples were fearful of death in this situation. This is quite surprising since at least seven of them were probably fishermen and quite used to stormy weather. It's good to know that they were human like us.

Yet while in that state of panic, they did something that we can learn from: they went to the only person they knew that could help them, Jesus. He saw their fear and dealt with it, firstly by calming the storm and secondly by talking openly and frankly about death and the certainty of eternal life. "

LAP 2

Thought:
Jesus' claims and promises about eternal life

Total Time: 10 minutes

The card trail
9 minutes

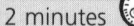

Prepare some cards as illustrated in the example below, so that when the lines are followed, the Bible verses can be discovered. Use John 6:40; 8:47 or 11:25. Shuffle each set of cards and give a different set to each team. See which team can form the Bible verse the quickest. Make sure all three of the verses are completed at this point, and once completed stay completed for the rest of the session

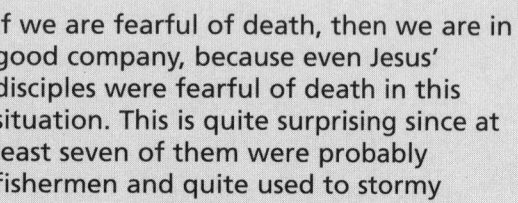

I	AM	THOUGH	HE	DIES
AND	THE	LIVE	EVEN	JOHN
THE	RESURRECTION	WILL	11	VERSE
LIFE	BELIEVES	IN	ME	25
WHOEVER				

Commentator
1 minute

" Jesus certainly left us with some wonderful claims and promises, but many quite rightly ask, 'How can we be sure that what he says is true?'

Ask if anyone knows of any examples of promises Jesus made, then either read or retell one of the following incidents:

a) Jairus' daughter (Mark 5:21–42)
b) The son of the widow of Nain (Luke 7:11–17)
c) The raising of Lazarus (John 11:1–44)

Explain that Jesus was to prove even more convincingly that what he claimed was true. Read out Matthew 20:17–19 and compare the passage with Mark 5:6–16.

Through the biblical accounts we see that Jesus fulfilled his claims completely and as such we can have total confidence and assurance that:

a) There is life after death;
b) We can receive that gift of eternal life through believing and following Jesus. "

LAP 3

Thought: What is heaven/eternal life like then?

Total Time: 21 minutes

Art work — 10 minutes

Ask the group to draw a picture of what they think heaven will be like and then select some members to explain to the others what they have drawn and why.

Commentator — 1 minute

"Explain that many people have many different ideas as to what heaven is like, some of which may be based on what the Bible says, some may not be. So what can we be certain of in regards to heaven? What does the Bible tell us about it?"

Activity sheet — 10 minutes

Ask the group to complete the activity sheet entitled 'What is heaven like then?' (see page 64). Go through the answers using the following notes to help you:

The Bible doesn't give the exact location of heaven, but what it does say is that heaven is where God is, where he will dwell with those whose names are written in the book of life and those who Jesus calls his own, ie those who have chosen to believe and respond to Jesus. Through Jesus these people are and will be pure as well as being free from all imperfection, pain and grief. They will enjoy being in God's presence, worshipping and serving him, which will be a great joy to them and not a bind. The Bible mentions nothing about us playing harps or sitting on clouds but shows that it is a place of indescribable beauty and enjoyment, wonderful in every way.

Chequered Flag — 5 minutes

Sum up the session by reiterating how good God is. He sent Jesus to earth on a special mission so that he could ultimately offer the gift of eternal life to all and therefore take away the fear relating to death.

Read Luke 23:39–43. Explain that as with any gift, eternal life needs to be accepted. Unfortunately some people in this world can be like the thief on the cross who shouted insults at Jesus and as such can miss out on eternal life because they choose not to trust, believe and follow him. Yet those who choose to be like the other thief on the cross who believed and trusted Jesus can be assured, just like he was, that they will receive eternal life. The question is who are we most like?

If appropriate, pray and leave space for any feedback from this final challenge.

On the Podium — 2 minutes

Add all the scores up throughout the session and award the prizes for *Dead or alive, Make a coffin, Help the boat's sinking!* and *The card trail*.

Lap of Honour — 8 minutes

a) Read Revelation 21:10 – 22:5 to the group. Ask them to imagine what heaven could be like. Ask them to write thank you prayers, thanking God for wanting to share the splendour of heaven with each of us.

b) Obtain a copy of the album *Addicted to Jesus* by Carmen, and play the track 'The Third Heaven', which is all about a near death experience. Use this to focus on the reality of eternal life.

13 What is heaven like then?

PART 1

Match the correct Bible verse to the question that it helps to answer.

...Now Gods home is with mankind! He will live with them, and they shall be his people. God himself will be with them, and he will be their God.
Revelation 21:3

He who sits on the throne will protect them with his presence.
Revelation 7:15

But nothing that is impure will enter the city, nor anyone who does shameful things or tells lies.
Revelation 21:27

Only those whose names are written in the Lamb's book of the living will enter the city
Revelation 21:27

He will wipe away all tears from their eyes. There will be no more death, no more grief or crying or pain. The old things have disappeared.
Revelation 21:4

That is why they stand before Gods throne and serve him day and night in his temple.
Revelation 7:15

A What will we do in heaven?
B Where is heaven?
C Who will be there?
D What will there not be in heaven?
E Who will not be there?
F Who will look after us?

PART 2

Find the answers to the clues below in the above verses. Place the answers in the grid to find the word which completes the final sentence.

Not clean _____
Another word for humanity _____
A stage people pass through before heaven _____
Parts of the body you see through _____
To put others first, means to _____
A large town _____
Something royalty may sit on _____
Not dead _____
An animal sacrificed by the Jews _____
Unhappy streams of water _____
A collection of pages form a what? _____
Someone who does not tell the truth does what? _____
A holy religious building? _____

Heaven is .... because it's so wonderful and beyond our imagination!

[For a further glimpse read Revelation 21:10-22:5].

Suffering

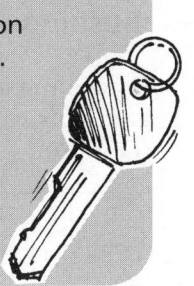

Qualifying

Why God allows people to suffer or experience hardship is one of the most common objections/questions that people have about Christianity in today's society. Such a questioner may have a negative view of God, maybe seeing him as weak, impotent and uncaring. This session seeks to tackle this topic by sensitively showing group members that God is full of love, compassion and understanding; willing to share in our sufferings and meet our deepest needs.

Sensitivity will be required for this session because suffering/hardship effects us all. The key for a successful time is not to ream off pat dogmatic answers but to listen to where the group members are coming from and then sensitively reveal the goodness of God in the way that he directs you.

Starting Grid
(10 minutes)

Through this section aim to show that there are many ways in which people suffer and experience hardship.

A Descriptive capers
(10 minutes)

Play a form of the well-known board game *Taboo*. Prepare a range of cards with the following words on, the keyword being in bold text.

Accident	Hurt, Hospital, Ambulance
Depression	Sad, Suicide, Tranquillisers
Disability	Wheelchair, Help, Charity
Disappointment	Sad, Let-down, Hurt
Divorce	Married, Separated, Court
Homelessness	Live, Street, Beg
Homesickness	Miss, Ill, Sad
Injustice	Unfair, Innocent, Wrong
Loneliness	Alone, Partner, Sad
Malnutrition	Food, Hunger, Die
Natural disasters	Earthquake, Hurricane, People
Pain	Hurt, Hit, Cry
Persecution	Unfair, Outsider, Picked-on
Poverty	Poor, Money, Little
Rejection	Unloved, Unwanted, Sad
Sickness	Ill, Hospital, Doctor
Temptation	Devil, Evil, Sin
Terrorism	Bomb, Frighten, Kill
Unemployment	Job, Dole, Benefit
War	Countries, Fight, Kill

Place the cards in a box face down and then split the group members into two teams. Each team is to select a describer, who in turn has 30 seconds to work through as many cards as possible. They try and describe the key word to their team without using any of the words or derivatives on the given card. Their team in the mean time shout out their responses to the descriptions given until they correctly guess the key word on the card. One point is scored for each key word guessed correctly.

B Consequences
(10 minutes)

Give each member a piece of paper and a pen, then read the following passage to them. When you get to a section in bold, each member is to continue the story in the way described, then fold over their answer and pass their paper along to another person. Once you've completed the story, re-read the passage to discover what strange happenings occurred to Billy, the main character.

'Billy couldn't remember what happened. One moment he was **1) an action** down the street, the next he **2) describe an accident he had** and so he was rushed off into hospital. The doctors performed many tests on Billy including **3) describe a test the doctors did** and finally made a diagnosis. They discovered that he had **4) describe a disease/problem**. He couldn't believe it. He knew that his girlfriend wouldn't want to go out with him now. He therefore felt **5) a suitable emotion**. He then learnt that his condition affected his **6) a clean part of his anatomy**, which blew his chances of serving in the army. All his dreams of war, stopping terrorism, injustice, helping the malnourished and refugees of the world were shattered like a **7) something breakable**. However, while he was feeling sorry for himself, he was befriended by Samantha. She was beautiful and had a face like **8) a suitable description** but was in hospital because **9) a suitable reason**. She didn't laugh at his misfortune but helped him to overcome his disability by the use of his **10) an object**.'

Thought:
How do we react in times of suffering/hardship?

Total Time: up to 20 minutes

'Rushing to Jesus' game

18 minutes

Before the game, make the following game board on a long strip of paper to be laid on the floor.

Q	T1	T2	P	Q	Q	Q	T3	P	T4	P	T5	Q	Jesus
1	2	3	4	5	6	7	8	9	10	11	12	13	14	15	16	17	18

For each team prepare six general knowledge questions. Buy a big bag of sweets and the materials needed for the task.

Ask the group to imagine that they are living at the time of Jesus and a friend becomes seriously ill. There are no hospitals but you've heard of a man called Jesus who heals people. With no hesitation you seek to get your sick friend to Jesus as quickly as possible. In the game you will have a team to help you. Teams take turns to roll a dice and move as follows: throw 1 or 4 – move 1 space, 2 or 5 – move 2 spaces, 3 or 6 – move 3 spaces.

Along their way they may fall on one of the following spaces:

Q= A question. When a team lands on this space, they are asked one of your previously prepared general knowledge questions. If they get it right they move one space forward, if they get it wrong they stay where they are.

P= A prize. All team members are given a sweet.

T= A task. The team that lands on this space unlocks a task which is to be completed by everyone in all teams. The first team to complete the task successfully is awarded a rest card, which can be played on a future turn to nominate an opposing team to miss one go. The tasks are as follows:

Task 1 Your injured man has a headache. Which team can be the most still and quiet for 30 seconds?

Task 2 Two of your team mates break their arms. Which team can be the first to make them slings, made from toilet tissue?

Task 3 On the way you get hungry and need food. Which team can make the longest shopping list with items only beginning with A, B and C?

Task 4 You get mugged by bandits from another team. Which team can make the best portrait of an opposing team member in 1 minute?

Task 5 Each person wants to see Jesus. Which team can be the first to arrange their members in height order?

NB The tasks are numbered. Once a task has been played it cannot be played again. Any team which lands on a played task space should treat it as a blank space.

Once completed, read a story about Jesus healing someone, eg Matthew 9:1–8 or Mark 7:31–37. Alternatively, show the story of Bartimaeus from the *Chattabox* video, published by Scripture Union (10 minutes).

Commentator

2 minutes

"How do we react when we face suffering/hardship? Are we like the person we've just read about who chose to run to God for help?

Or do we do the opposite? Do we turn our back on God and blame him for the trouble we experience and harbour negative, hostile feelings towards him? Depending upon our situation we may feel quite justified about doing this, but is God really so bad?"

Thought:
What is God like?

Total Time: 25 minutes

Blockbusters

20 minutes

Make an enlarged copy of the board below and photocopy the questions from the activity sheet (see page 68). Split the group into teams and assign a colour to them. (Two or more teams can play this version at once.)

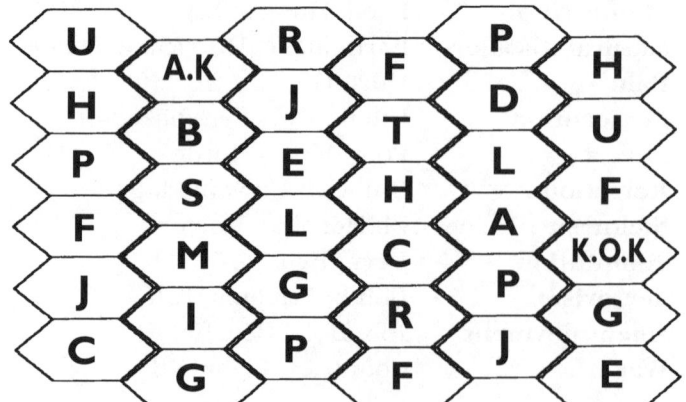

Start by picking a letter from the board and asking the corresponding question. The first team to put up their hand and answer correctly, gets that space filled in with their colour.

They then choose a letter from the board and the corresponding question is asked once again to everyone and so on. The winning team is the one with the most spaces coloured in. (If a team manages to connect the top to the bottom or the left to the right with their colour, it doesn't mean that they have won, but it does mean that they will receive 5 extra space bonuses at the end.)

If a team answers incorrectly, the next team on your right has a chance to answer. If they don't answer correctly, pass the question on to the next team on the right and so on. If no one can answer the question correctly, tell them the answer and then pick a letter as at the beginning of the game.

All of the clues have second clues. These are useful if your group finds the clues hard.

Commentator   5 minutes

"What is God like? On one hand he is almighty, powerful and to be respected (Psalm 50), yet on the other he deeply yearns to have a quality friendship with us.

God is overwhelmingly good (Psalm 11:5), he's big enough to take our outbursts of anger, hurt and resentment. However instead of being a punch bag, ie just being on the receiving end of our blows, he wants to actively come alongside us and help us through the situation that we are finding hard to cope with. But how does he know what suffering/hardship is like?"

Thought:
God understands our suffering through Jesus

Total Time: 12 minutes

Suffering activity sheet   10 minutes

Photocopy the activity sheet (page 70). All the words are from different translations of Isaiah 52:13 – 53:12 and help to express the suffering/hardship that Jesus went through. If you feel your group will quietly listen to the whole of this reading then read it to them. If not, the activity sheet should bring accross the desired point or show a crucifixion scene from a video about Jesus, then ask the group members for words which describe how he suffered.

Commentator   2 minutes

"God knows what it is like to experience hardship through the pain that Jesus endured throughout his trial and crucifixion – suffering that most of us would choose to avoid. Jesus had that choice too, as he knew of his fate before he was arrested (Matthew 8:21). Yet he chose to suffer so that we could become friends with this wonderful God we've been learning about today (Romans 5:18,19). This means that he is able to meet our innermost needs during hard times, if we choose to seek his help."

Chequered Flag   5 minutes

We may still struggle with questions such as 'Why me?', 'Why don't I get better?' or 'Why did someone I care for die?', and although we can suggest some answers, often we just have to admit that we don't know the reason why someone suffers in the way they do. What we do know is that we have a God who understands (Hebrews 4:13). Focussing on what we *do* know, rather than on the 'Why?' question.

Finish this summary by reminding the group what a great caring God we do have by either reading the famous Christian passage 'Footprints' or by reading Psalm 121.

On the Podium   5 minutes

Count up the team points and award prizes accordingly.

Lap of Honour   10 minutes

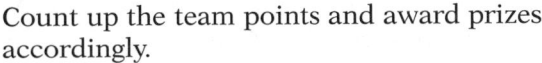

Use this time to allow the group members to express what they've learnt about God being so loving and caring by either:

a) Asking them to draw a picture describing how they view God now;

b) Writing a thank you note/prayer to God expressing their feelings;

c) Asking the group members to create a rap which expresses the goodness of God. This could either be made up from scratch or developed from a hymn/chorus. All that is needed is a taped rap beat (which can be easily recorded from most electronic keyboards) and a lot of imagination.

BLOCKBUSTER QUESTIONS

1.
a) What A, when used to describe God, means to be there when you need him, ready to give you time?
b) When there is an empty seat A........ then you can sit down.
(Available)

2.
a) God loves to B........ his people. What B, which means to make happy, best describes what God loves to do?
b) We often use this word when someone sneezes.
(Bless)

3.
a) God can be described as never C........ This means to stay the same and to be steadfast.
b) This C rhymes with ranging.
(Changing)

4.
a) What C used to describe God means to make something new/bring into being?
b) In seven days God C....... the earth.
(Creator/Created)

5.
a) What D used to describe God means to protect from attack?
b) You can usually find one in a football team.
(Defender)

6.
a) What E used to describe God means always has been, always is and always will be? It also means infinite and everlasting.
b) This E rhymes with maternal.
(Eternal)

7.
a) What E used to describe God means to be in all places, all of the time?
b) This E also loosely rhymes with feathery chair.
(Everywhere)

8.
a) What F used to describe God means to be a parent responsible for their child's welfare?
b) Opposite of mother.
(Father)

9.
a) What F used to describe God means someone who is true to their word, keeps their promises and stays with you in all circumstances?
b) You often hear of a dog being called a F........ friend.
(Faithful)

10.
a) What F used to describe God means someone who forgets about the wrong things that have been done to them?
b) When you apologise to someone you expect them to F........ you.
(Forgive)

11.
a) What F used to describe God means to be your close companion?
b) This F rhymes with send, bend and lend.
(Friend)

12.
a) What G used to describe God means to give freely in abundance?
b) This G is the opposite of stingy.
(Generous)

13.
a) What G used to describe God means to be mild, quiet, soft and soothing?
b) This G rhymes with lentil.
(Gentle)

14.
a) What G used to describe God means someone who shows the way forward?
b) This G rhymes with dried, fried and lied
(Guide)

15.
a) What H used to describe God means to make better, cure and to make whole?
b) This H rhymes with Sheila.
(Healer)

16.
a) What H used to describe God means to assist, aid, support someone in need?
b) This H rhymes with Shelter.
(Helper)

17.
a) What H used to describe God means to set apart, without blemish and free from wrong doing?
b) A polo could also be described as this.
(Holy)

18.
a) What I used to describe God means unconquerable and never can be defeated?
b) This word sounds like invisible.
(Invincible)

BLOCKBUSTER QUESTIONS

19 a) What J used to describe God means to be envious of other relationships?
b) This J rhymes with 'tell us'.
(Jealous)

20 a) What J used to describe God means someone who makes desicions about whether someone is innocent or guilty?
b) You'll find one of these in court.
(Judge)

21 a) What J means upright and fair?
b) This J rhymes with trust.
(Just)

22 a) What AK used to describe God means to be aware of, to understand everything?
The K rhymes with showing.
(All-knowing)

23 a) What KOK used to describe God means to be the supreme royal ruler over all authority here on earth?
b) You don't often hear God described as a Queen!
(King of Kings)

24 a) What L used to describe God means to hear what you say?
b) You use your ears to do this.
(Listener)

25 a) What L used to describe God means to have a strong affection for another, being more concerned about that person's welfare than their own?
b) Many L......... celebrate on St Valentine's day.
(Lover)

26 a) What M used to describe God means to be compassionate, coming alongside the needy and sharing their prioblem?
b) This M rhymes with Percival.
(Merciful)

27 a) What P used to describe God means to be quiet and calm?
b) This P rhymes with cease.
(Peace)

28 a) What P used to describe God means someone with great strength and might with the ability to act upon anyone or anything?
b) A fast car has a P........ engine.
(Powerful)

29 a) What P used to describe God means to supply and equip one's needs?
b) This P rhymes with 'no rides'.
(Provides)

30 a) What P used to describe God means without defect or fault?
b) A score of 100% is classed as a P........ score.
(Perfect)

31 a) What R used to describe God means to be one's shelter, protector and hide away?
b) Your bedroom may be classed as your R........ from your parents.
(Refuge)

32 a) What R used to describe God means dependable, trustworthy and someone who always carrys out their promises?
b) This R ryhmes with buyable.
(Reliable)

33 a) What S used to describe God means rescuer, deliverer and redeemer?
b) A hero who has saved someone from dying is often called a S........
(Saviour)

34 a) What T used to describe God means to be honest, without telling a lie?
b) This T sounds like 'Ruth fell'.
(Truthful)

35 a) What U used to describe God means to be the only one of the kind, a one off item?
b) This U sounds like clinic.
(Unique)

36 a) What U used to describe God means to have no boundaries, no constraints or a certain supply of resources?
b) In some theme parks you pay once for an U........ amount of rides.
(Unlimited)

Suffering

Find the following words in the grid, all of which are used to describe the suffering that Jesus went through. They will either be horizontal, vertical, diagonal and backwards.

o	i	t	n	e	c	o	n	n	i	c	u	n
d	i	s	f	i	g	u	r	e	d	r	e	h
d	e	d	n	u	o	w	l	k	e	t	a	a
e	f	s	a	t	o	o	l	j	a	m	d	r
t	d	p	p	k	u	p	w	e	a	e	l	s
c	e	f	u	i	a	p	b	r	i	t	z	u
e	t	f	a	n	s	r	r	d	u	m	r	f
j	c	e	f	p	i	e	r	c	e	d	o	f
e	i	r	i	e	d	s	d	u	r	w	u	e
r	l	c	c	r	u	s	h	e	d	g	g	r
r	f	k	i	l	l	e	d	e	t	a	h	s
o	f	r	x	l	e	d	e	e	d	f	l	e
s	a	c	f	u	n	f	a	i	r	l	y	b

Afflicted	Beaten	Crushed	Cut
Despised	Died	Disfigured	Hated
Innocent	Killed	Marred	Oppressed
Pierced	Punished	Rejected	Roughly
Suffer	Unfairly	Wounded	

Evil and the Occult

Qualifying

This is an important issue to tackle with your group as they may come into contact with occult influences either directly or indirectly through the media and by listening to friends talk about their experiences.

Your first priority for this session is to gather as much prayer support as you can, as such a session can be full of hard questions, personal experiences and unwanted distractions.

While you don't need to be an expert in the field, it may be useful to read around the subject. Useful books can be obtained from Reachout Trust (0181 332 7785).

On a practical note keep the focus of attention on Jesus, avoid creating too much interest in occult practices.

Starting Grid

(upto 18 minutes)

A Connections quiz

7 minutes

REW ◀◀ Make the following clues below and place them onto cards, then split the group into teams.

Show each card in order, one at a time. After each one ask the group if they can guess what the connection between them all is. For the team which correctly guesses the answer of 'evil', award the given points.

	Clues	Points
1	Cut a newspaper cutting of an act of evil, eg murder.	20
2	Draw a picture of fire.	18
3	Draw a picture of a snake.	16
4	Cut out a newspaper item about unfairness.	14
5	Write the name of a horror film.	12
6	Fill in the blanks T _ _ PT _ _ I _ N.	10
7	Cut out a newspaper item about greed.	8
8	Draw a pitchfork.	6
9	Sounds like Saturn.	4
10	Write the word WEEVIL.	2

B Monster fun

10 minutes

Split the group into teams and see which team can make the best monster out of one of their team-mates, in the time given. Provide a large amount of collective materials for the teams to use. Such materials may include newspaper, loo rolls, sellotape, cardboard, face packs, face paints, peanut butter etc.

Commentator

1 minute

"At present there seems to be a lot of interest in the supernatural in all types of media presentation. However, there's not much talk about God. The focus seems to be on practices which claim to reveal hidden truths. These often look to be attractive, exciting and fun, yet are they all they promise to be?"

Thought:
Looks can be deceptive

Total Time: 17 minutes

Minefield

12 minutes

Draw a blank grid on card or OHP acetate containing 5 columns and 12 rows. Split the group into teams. Explain that they have managed to find their way into the centre of a minefield and now have to find a way out of it, ie from the top to the bottom of the grid.

Start by asking each team which space they would like to choose on the first row. Once each team has picked a space, compare their choice to the master grid on page 74 to see what needs to happen to each team. Then continue down the grid.

If a team lands on a blank space, it means they have successfully chosen a mine free spot and they are safe till their next turn.

If a team lands on an X space it means that they have hit a mine and are injured. Each team starts with 120 points. For every hit they lose 10 points from their score.

If a team lands on a Q space, it means that they

have hit a mine but it's touch and go as to whether it detonates. If they answer the given question correctly they will be safe, if not then the mine will detonate, causing them to lose ten points from their total score.

If a team chooses the same question space, ask each team the same question. Get them to write their answer down and reveal it at the same time as the next team.

Each question requires the team to decide whether or not the creature or activity mentioned is potentially harmful to humans or unsuspecting creatures.

Don't feel you have to ask the questions in the given order, but please make sure you include all the occult practices. After you mention they are harmful, you may be asked why. Explain to the enquirers that all will be revealed later on in the session.

The winning team is the one with the most life points left at the end.

Commentator

5 minutes

"Talk about the principal of a mouse trap. These traps work by enticing the mouse or rat to it by the food you lay upon it. If they then choose to touch and taste it, they will find that the food hides a deadly surprise.

This principle certainly applies to those practices which claim to reveal hidden truths, often referred to as 'occult' practices. 'Occult' means 'to try to reveal secrets beyond man's natural understanding'.

In Minefield, a few of these practices were mentioned such as horoscope's, tarot cards, palm reading, seances and ouija boards. Ask if any of the group have come across such practices and allow time for them to briefly share any experiences. Ask the group if they feel such practices are harmful or not.

Explain that there are two sources of hidden information and knowledge, supernatural help or guidance: God and Satan. The reason why occult practices can be so harmful is that they turn the participant away from God and encourage contact with satan."

Thought:
What is Satan like?

Total Time: up to 13 minutes

Satan revealed activity sheet
10 minutes

Photocopy enough activity sheets (see page 75) for everyone to have one copy each.

Commentator

 3 minutes

"Satan, believe it or not, is believed to have been a high-ranking angel who became proud and wanted to be like God (Ezekiel 28:12–19; Isaiah 14:12–15). He was thrown out of heaven and took a third of the angels with him (Revelation 12:4). He now stands in total opposition to God and seeks to destroy, harm and damage all that God cares about, which includes us!"

Thought:
To see Jesus' reaction to people harmed by Satan

Total Time: 23 minutes

Active story
up to 20 minutes

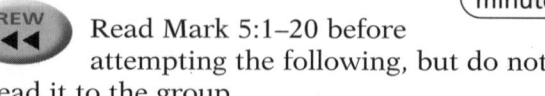 Read Mark 5:1–20 before attempting the following, but do not read it to the group.

The point of this activity is to get the group members involved in the Bible incident by using many smaller activities to gradually reveal the facts about the incident. Split the group into teams, then use the following as your script:

1) Give everyone a piece of paper. They have 2 minutes to make a boat from it. Each team is to then pick the best and enter it for judging. Award team points.

The incident we're looking at happened immediately after Jesus had shown his power over nature by calming a storm on Lake Galilee (Mark 4:35–41). The disciples reached the other side of the lake and touched down in the territory of Gerasa (v 1). They were met by a man who lived among the burial caves and tombs, who had an evil spirit within him (v 2).

2) Give each team a sheet of old wallpaper and marker pens to do a life-sized drawing of what they

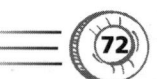

think the man looked like. Give them five minutes to complete the task and then award points accordingly.

This man was seriously disturbed. He often wandered among the tombs and through the hills, screaming and cutting himself with stones. Consequently, he was placed in chains (vs 3–5).

3) See which team can mummify one of their team members the best using toilet tissue in two minutes. (NB Keep the tied up member in their shackles for the next activity!) Award points accordingly.

However the man was so disturbed that he kept breaking out of them and in fact nobody could keep him chained up any more (v 3).

4) See which tied up team member can do the best dramatic piece of escapology. Award points accordingly.

This man saw Jesus and even though he was a long way off, ran, fell down on his knees before him and screamed in a loud voice, 'Jesus, Son of the Most High God! What do you want with me? For God's sake, I beg you, don't punish me!'

5) Find out which team can shout this verse the loudest and award points accordingly.

The reason why the man reacted like this is that Jesus was commanding the evil spirit within him to leave. In fact, this man didn't have just one evil spirit – there were many inside him. They knew Jesus was the Son of God and knew that they would have to leave the man. They begged Jesus to send them into a nearby herd of pigs.

6) Find out which team can make one of their members into the best pig, using just newspaper and tape. They have two minutes.

Jesus sent the evil spirits into the pigs who then rushed down the mountain side, over a cliff and were drowned (v 13). Those tending the pigs rushed off and told the local people what happened. They came out to see the man for themselves, who of course was clothed, in his right mind and totally cured (vs 14–16).

The people were so scared by this they asked Jesus to leave. The healed man desperately wanted to follow Jesus, but Jesus asked him to stay and tell his fellow countrymen what had happened to him, which he did (vs 17–20).

Add the scores and put them towards the final total.

Commentator 3 minutes

"The man in the story had been harmed by Satan. We don't know how but we know that he had become seriously disturbed. Jesus wasn't intimidated by the man, but showed a great amount of care, concern and love for him.

The way Jesus chose to help him was to deal with the root of the problem – the evil spirits, real beings who are under Satan's command. Notice they were scared of Jesus.

Point out that Satan isn't the evil equal opposite of God. God is by far more powerful – after all, God is the Creator and Satan is just a fallen created angel!"

Chequered Flag 10 minutes

Although friends and the media may portray occult practices as attractive, exciting and fun, they can be harmful to us. This is because they start to put us in contact with Satan and his followers who have the express intention of harming us, so that they can ultimately harm God. God knows this and that is why his instructions and advice are very clear in the Bible: we are not to be involved in them.

However, if we have made a mistake in the past and messed with such practices, it's good to know that we have a God who is much more powerful than Satan and can heal us of all harmful effects, if we choose to turn and follow him alone.

Consolidate the session by asking each person to design a poster which expresses a point that they have learnt. It may be a 'Do Not Touch' poster or simply a drawing of Jesus being more powerful than Satan.

On the Podium 5 minutes

Calculate the total scores for each team, from the following items: *Connections quiz*, *Monster fun*, *Minefield* and *Active story*.

Lap of Honour 10 minutes

So that you can focus on Christ's power/victory over Satan, read Colossians 2:15 and in teams ask them to think what that might have looked like. Ask them to dramatise it and then show their completed piece to everyone.

Minefield Master grid

	1	2	3	4	5
A	Q	X	Q		X
B	Q	Q	X	X	
C	X	X		Q	Q
D	Q	X	Q	X	
E		Q	Q	X	X
F		X	X	Q	Q
G	X		Q	Q	X
H	Q	X	Q	X	
I		X	X	Q	Q
J	X	Q	Q	X	

Questions

1 A green discus fish — non-harmful
2 A puff adder — harmful
3 The plant Toxicodendron Radicans (poison ivy) — harmful
4 Horoscopes — harmful
5 Tarot cards — harmful
6 Chilopoda (centipedes) — non-harmful
7 Palm reading — harmful
8 Electrophorus electricus (electric eel) — harmful
9 Sphagnum (moss) — non-harmful
10 A swallow tail butterfly — non-harmful
11 Carum petroselinum (parsley) — non-harmful
12 Annelids (eg earthworms) — non-harmful
13 Seances — harmful
14 Ouija Boards — harmful
15 Giant tortoise — non-harmful
16 Pitcher plants (plants which trap insects) — harmful
17 The plant Dionaea Musciplua (Venus fly trap) — harmful
18 The Merino ram — non-harmful
19 The Portuguese man of war jellyfish — harmful
20 Gila monsters (venomous lizard) — harmful

An alternative to this game is simply to split the group into twos or threes and ask the above questions to see how many they get right.

SATAN revealed

In the wordsearch below, find the answers to the descriptions of Satan we find in the Bible.

d	t	o	n	a	t	a	s
l	r	i	v	e	n	u	i
r	a	i	e	n	e	q	r
o	p	r	n	o	p	d	u
w	p	e	o	l	r	k	l
s	e	r	t	i	e	w	e
i	r	e	a	v	s	h	r
h	v	d	n	e	e	u	o
t	d	r	g	c	n	n	f
f	e	u	e	t	e	c	d
o	v	m	l	u	m	l	a
e	i	o	p	m	y	e	r
c	l	s	e	t	d	a	k
n	l	i	a	r	e	n	n
i	e	l	i	o	n	r	e
r	e	s	u	c	c	a	s
p	g	b	e	s	f	u	s

NAMES

1	The D _ _ _ L	(Matthew 4:1)
2	The E _ E _ Y	(1 Peter 5:8)
3	E V _ _ O _ E	(Matthew 6:13)
4	P _ _ N _ _ O F T _ _ S W _ _ _ D	(John 12:31 NIV)
5	S _ _ _ N	(Matthew 16:23
6	U N _ L _ _ N	(2 Corinthians 6:17)
7	The L _ _ R	(John 8:44)
8	The T _ M P _ _ _	(1 Thessalonians 3:5, NIV)
9	The A C C _ _ E _	(Revelation 12:10, NIV)
10	The M _ R D _ _ _ R	(John 8:44)
11	The S _ _ P _ _ T	(Revelation 20:2)
12	ONE WHO AIMS TO T _ _ P YOU	(2 Timothy 2:26)
13	An A _ G _ _	(2 Corthinthians 11:14)
14	Like a L _ _ N	(1 Peter 5:8)

Temptation

Qualifying

Temptation affects us all and since there are so many unhealthy attractions for young people in today's society, it is a highly relevant topic. This session seeks to encourage the group members to realise the source of temptation and to encourage them to resist temptation to sin.

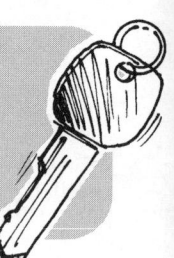

Starting Grid
(10 minutes minimum)

A Enticing appetisers — 10 minutes

Bring a selection of ingredients for each team to use. They have a certain time to make the best sandwich, pizza, cake etc, using their imagination (and no recipe books!). Once each team has made their item, invite up to three individual people to judge: one to find the most attractively smelling; one to find the most attractively tasting and one who seeks to find the most eye-pleasing creation. Award points accordingly.

B Making things attractive — 10 minutes

Often we are tempted or enticed when we are attracted to something. The following activity ideas suggest ways to explore that point. They can either be used independently or in conjunction with one another.

i) Make an advert

Give each team either an unattractive object or a made up word which doesn't sound that nice eg, a gobulator or grot grabber. The teams are given five minutes to firstly decide what their object does and to work on an advert for it. These are then either video-ed or shown straight to the other group members.

ii) Surprise, surprise!

Pick two volunteers from the group and blindfold them. Then pick three other helpers who are each given a tempting description of a mystery item to read. One of those items is a treat; the others are not so pleasant. Once the descriptions have been read, the blindfolded volunteers then choose which item they wish to pick and sample their choice item while still blindfolded. Below are the first three descriptions. Make some more up yourself and play the game for longer if you want to.

Description A (A cream cake)
Go on – be naughty and indulge yourself in my incredibly nice surprise. One nibble on my item will give you an appetite for more!

Description B (A custard pie)
Don't clown about considering the other two items, pick mine. Once you feel my soft, warm, gentle item next to you, you'll be desperate that others share in your good fortune also.

Description C (A melted ice cream)
My delectable item is the coolest of them all. No need to get hot and bothered as my item will melt all your cares away!

Commentator

1 minute

"Temptation is a phenomena which we all experience. It's a serious issue, because if we are not aware as to where temptation comes from and how to handle it, then we could find ourselves in a potentially damaging situation."

Thought:
How do we handle temptation?

Total Time: 12 minutes

Questionnaire — 10 minutes

Give out photocopies of the temptations questionnaire (see page 79) asking the group members to indicate their most likely reaction to each temptation.

Read out the points to be awarded for each answer and then ask them to add up their scores.

1 a) 5   b) 10   c) 2
2 a) 2   b) 10   c) 5
3 a) 2   b) 10   c) 5
4 a) 10   b) 2   c) 5

5	a) 10	b) 2	c) 5
6	a) 5	b) 10	c) 2
7	a) 5	b) 2	c) 10
8	a) 2	b) 5	c) 10
9	a) 10	b) 2	c) 5
10	a) 2	b) 5	c) 10

Read out the following comments:

20–45

You must be living life in the fast lane, living for thrills, doing a whole lot of taking but not much giving. It may all catch up with you. Save yourself a lot of hassle and start wising up and seeing the potential consequences of your actions.

46–79

Depending how the mood takes you, you either choose to steer a middle course through life's choices or behave quite recklessly. Continue to consider the options available to you, and realise that you don't have to join the crowd to be a valuable, fun-loving party dude!

80–100

You are learning to make wise choices. Keep it up and work on the areas in your life which you know are weak to temptation.

Commentator
2 minutes

" As we have just seen we all react to temptation differently, depending on the temptation and the situation we find ourselves in. Why is that? Is it OK to succumb to temptation as long as nobody else gets hurt?

Some may think that temptation isn't a big deal, but how do people in the Bible react to it and why? "

LAP 2

Thought:
Bible characters who resisted temptation

Total Time: 23 minutes

Get away Joseph
10 minutes

Either read Genesis 39:1–12 or retell the story in your own words. To consolidate this story, produce a board similar to the following on page 80.

Ask for two players – one to be A, Potiphar's wife and one B, Joseph. Each player has one dice and on your command start rolling them at the same time, thus moving around the board route (without moving diagonally). The idea of the game is for player A to try and catch player B before Joseph has made his way to the exit.

This is a fast-moving game. Play it until most people have had a go, or until you see people getting bored.

Commentator
2 minutes

" Joseph was a handsome man (v 6b) and as a result attracted the attention of Potiphar's wife (verse 7). In today's society Joseph may be seen as odd, passing over such an invitation, but he had chosen to follow and serve God (v 9) which meant that pleasing God came first. "

The temptation of Jesus
8 minutes

Either show a relevant clip from a film about Jesus or read Luke 4:1–13 from a modern Bible translation, eg The Message.

Commentator
3 minutes

" Here we first of all discover who's at the source of all temptation: the devil. We also discover why he chooses to tempt people (so that he can try and pull them away from loving, following, serving and pleasing God). But in this instance, even though the devil tried to cause Jesus to disobey, doubt and test his Father, he couldn't. As a result of Jesus' trust in his Father and God's help through the Holy Spirit (v 1), the devil left without success, until another opportune time (v 13, NIV). "

LAP 3

Thought:
Resisting temptation is not the weak option

Total Time: 11 minutes

Open the box
10 minutes

Have ten numbered boxes drawn on a large board. In each box write either 'Forfeit', 'Good prize' or 'Booby prize'. Cover each box with a card showing just its number.

For each contestant go through the following:

a) Ask them three general knowledge questions from a list you've prepared earlier. If they succeed in getting at least two correct, then go on to the boxes. If they fail they are out of the game.

b) Ask the contestant to select a numbered box. Explain that behind each box there is either a good prize, a booby prize or a forfeit.

c) As game host you then try and tempt the contestant not to open the box by offering them an increasing amount of sweets. Some may choose to take the sweets; others will insist on opening the box.

d) If they choose to open the box, give them the contents, whether it be a prize or forfeit.

Commentator
1 minute

"Often it is thought that loving and following God and his ways is a soft, weak and a non-credible option. How much further from the truth can you get?! Just as the game helped to demonstrate choosing to give in to temptation is the weak/easy option, choosing to follow God takes strength, courage and guts.

Thankfully God doesn't leave us to struggle on our own as he promises to help us to resist temptation if we choose to turn to him."

LAP 4

Thought: God wants to help us in temptation

Total Time: 14 minutes

The wheel of fortune Bible verse quiz
12 minutes

Prepare beforehand a sheet with dashes representing individual letters of Hebrews 2:18 (like hangman), then number the dashes 1–70.

Split into teams and give a couple of sheets and pens to each team.

Each team then suggests a consonant (no vowels allowed). From your prepared sheet, read off the numbers where those consonants exist. Award one point for each letter placed and ten points bonus points for the first team to correctly guess the verse. The winning team is the one with the most points at the end of the time. In order for this game not to drag, continue to urge the teams along and don't repeat yourself when announcing positions of letters.

Commentator
2 minutes

"As we have seen, Jesus was tempted, but the Bible explains he always chose to obey and follow God, because he knew that was the best way (Hebrews 4:15) and because he received help from his Father. Jesus promises not to leave us alone to face temptations but will help us through them, often providing us with a way out (1 Corinthians 10:13). The question is, do we want a way out or not?"

Chequered Flag *8 minutes*

This is a challenge based on Joshua 24:14–16.

We have discovered that temptation affects us all because it is a tactic used by the devil to try and draw people away from the security of the loving arms of God, placing them in a potential position where he can cause harm. Jesus knew this and so resisted temptation. Jesus doesn't want us to be harmed and wants us follow him. He gives his followers help and power to resist falling into temptation, when they seek his help.

On the Podium *5 minutes*

Calculate the total scores for each team from the follow activities: *Enticing appetisers*, *Making things attractive*, *Get away Joseph* and *The wheel of fortune quiz*.

Lap of Honour *5 minutes*

Ask the members to write down the qualities that they expect to find in a faithful, loyal friend. Ask them to read some out and relate their answers to the way that God is faithful to us, by not letting us face temptation alone. Sum up the thoughts expressed with a prayer of thanksgiving.

Questionnaire

Read through the questions and choose the answers closest to what you would do.

1. Someone has left their brand new top fashion trainers in the sports changing room at your school. You've been after some exactly like this pair for ages. You look at them and discover they are your size. Do you...
   a) leave them where you found them
   b) take them to the lost property
   c) put them into your bag – after all finders, keepers?

2. Someone in your class lent you some money so that you could get some dinner, as you had left yours at home. You've promised to pay them back but both you and your friend have forgotten about it, until now. Do you...
   a) say nothing to remind your friend
   b) pay the money back
   c) have the money ready, just in case the friend asks?

3. You go to a friend's birthday party, where no adult is present. Everybody seems to be either drinking or smoking. You are encouraged to join in. Do you...
   a) join in
   b) refuse and stick to soft drinks
   c) phone the police/seek an adult?

4. You really want the latest CD of your favourite pop group but you haven't got enough money. You see some full CD boxes on the shelf, and you also notice that all the shop assistant are busy. Do you...
   a) walk out the shop without the CD
   b) walk out the shop with the CD
   c) get a friend to buy it and illegally copy it?

5. You've not managed to do some maths homework which you've been given a final deadline for. Do you...
   a) go into school, and speak to the maths teacher
   b) leave for school but don't turn up/go off with friends elsewhere
   c) fake a sickness so that you don't have to go to school?

6. Someone in your class is really disliked by some other class mates, who love taking the mick. This person's done something really stupid and is getting teased more than ever. Do you...
   a) say nothing
   b) try and stick up for them
   c) join in, taunting them?

7. You have a strong disagreement with someone in your school. Both of you lose your tempers. Do you...
   a) call the person all the names under the sun
   b) use your fists to communicate your anger
   c) make your point and walk away?

8. You see a tough year 11 person bully and extort money from a year 7 person. Do you...
   a) ignore the situation and turn away
   b) try and help out in the situation
   c) go and tell a teacher?

9. While your parents are out you use their PC to surf the internet. Do you...
   a) use it help you with your homework
   b) look at all the x-rated adult material
   c) play the most bloodthirsty games you can on it?

10. You are out with some older friends. Wanting a laugh, they find an unlocked car and want to take it out on a test drive. Do you...
    a) jump right on in and take the wheel
    b) ask them to drop you home
    c) refuse to join them?

Get away Joseph

Some may think that temptation isn't a big deal, but how do we find people in the Bible reacting to it and why?

ACTIVITY SHEET

Bad habits

Qualifying

Young people may not consider that they have any bad habits – habits such as biting one's nails or swearing may be classed as just a normal part of life. This session seeks to show that we all have qualities and habits which the Bible regards to be bad, and it encourages us to change. The session points out that it's very hard to change by our own efforts, and explains that real change only comes through having a relationship with Jesus.

Starting Grid

(up to 13 minutes)

A Nail-biting — 5 minutes

Split the group into teams and ask for one or two volunteers from each team. Provide each volunteer with a large lollipop and mark a line on it halfway down. Explain that people often bite their nails and that you want them to imagine that the lollipop that they have is a giant finger – the lollipop (above the marked line) being the nail. See who can be the first to eat the lollipop down to the line.

B The bleep machine — 5 minutes

Read an article from a newspaper on to a cassette tape but inbetween words record a series of beeps, as though someone has sworn eg, 'The BEEP BEEP postman was BEEP late at delivering the BEEP BEEP post'. Play the tape back to the group members and discover if anyone can correctly write out the article ignoring the beeps.

C I can't stop! — 7 minutes

Make up a story about someone and their habits, which keeps referring to certain key words/phrases eg, 'Gary had terrible bad habits like picking his nose and swearing...'. Tell everyone what the key words are to listen for. Explain to the group that as soon as they hear one of these words, they are to get out of their seat and run to the other side of the room and back again. The first one back will receive a point. Read your story, watch the group members get worn out, count up the points and discover who the winner is.

Commentator — 1 minute

"When we think of bad habits, we perhaps think about those that we have already mentioned such as biting one's nails, swearing and picking one's nose, but the Bible lists many other qualities which it regards as being bad habits, which we will look at now."

Thought:

To look at some of the bad habits listed in the Bible

Total Time: 31 minutes

Play your cards right — 20 minutes

Buy a pack of playing cards (preferably large ones) and write on the playing face of each, one bad habit found in the Bible. Use the following passages to help you to do this: Galations 5:19–21, Ephesians 5:3–5 and Colossians 3:5–10. Repeat some of the words so that all the cards have something written on them.

Split the group into teams and for each team place six cards in a row, face down on a board in front of the group. Each team then throws a dice. The team which rolls the highest number gets control of the game and moves first.

Turn over their first card and ask whether they would like to keep it or would like to change it for a randomly selected card from the remaining cards in the pack. (This only applies to the first card or when a team has stuck.) Whatever the number of the showing card may be, the team now has to decide whether the next card in the row is going to be higher or lower. After they have made their choice, reveal the next card in the row. If they are correct, ask if the next card in the row is also going to be higher or lower and so on. If they are wrong, then they lose all their cards (which have to be replaced on their next go). At this point the other teams can have a free go.

When a team has chosen a card correctly, they can choose to stick. This means that they can stop their go and allow teams to roll the dice again to see who will win control of the game. When this team receives control again, they can start from the card where they chose to stick, which they can choose to change if they want to. If after the point where they chose to stick they make a wrong decision, instead of all their cards being removed and them having to start from the beginning, they start from the card where they chose to stick.

The team who gets to the end of their row of cards first is the winner of that round. Play enough rounds for the group members to enter into the game. Throughout the game, continually mention the qualities found on each card.

Commentator
3 minutes

"Compile a list of all the negative qualities found in the passages and read them out.

Playing cards have different suits with different numbers on. The ones we just used not only had different suits and numbers but also had written on them different habits we find in the Bible. This was to show that often people try and grade habits in order of seriousness. For example, someone may think that swearing isn't that serious and so might class it as a 'grade 2' bad habit, whereas they may think that sexual immorality is a much worse habit and so class it as a 'grade 8' bad habit. However, the Bible regards all such bad habits as equal because they all spoil how God wants us to be and, most importantly, spoil our relationship with God (Colossians 3:6).

How does this make you feel? What qualities do you think that God wants to see in our life?"

Good habits

Write the positive qualities of Galations 5:22,23a on one side of an A4 piece of paper and on the other write out those listed in Colossians 3:12–14. Duplicate enough copies for the group members to have one between two, and cut these papers into ten segments each. Put these segments into envelopes and give one to each pair, together with an OHP acetate.

The teams are to construct the A4 piece of paper on the OHP acetate to form the positive qualities found in the passages. The first pair to do this are the winners. (The OHP acetate is provided so that the team can see the qualities on both sides of the A4 piece of paper.)

Commentator
3 minutes

"Read these qualities out to the group and ask them to think about the degree to which these qualities are seen in their life. Ask them to consider whether more of the bad or the good qualities are evident in their life. God wants us to be like him and reflect the qualities he possesses. 'For all of us this means that there are things in our lives which need changing', 2 Corinthians 3:18."

Thought:
It's easier to solve a problem with help than to solve it on your own.

Total Time: 20 minutes

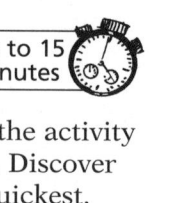

A Gearing for a problem?
up to 15 minutes

 Split into groups of different sizes. Give each group a copy of the activity sheet (see page 84) and a pair of scissors. Discover which group can solve the problem the quickest.

(Answer: These gears should go on the following axles: A=small, B=medium, C=large, D=medium, E=small, F=small, G=medium, H=large, I=medium and J=small)

Commentator
5 minutes

"Ask the groups whether they would feel that the problem was better tackled as a team or not. Comment on their actions which you observed during the activities.

Bring the discussion around to problems generally and ask the group whether they feel that problems are solved better on your own or with the help of others. Explain that the early Christians soon realised that problems were better shared and tackled together rather than their own. Read Galatians 6:1,2.

In the same way, when we realise that we have bad habits in our life, the best way we can deal with them is to gain help and strength from those who care about us – especially God.

Peter, one of Jesus' disciples, is a classic example of how God can work with someone to change their bad habits to good. "

So Jesus had made a good choice of friend after all. With the help of the Holy Spirit, Peter was able to change: his bad habits were changed for the good. Ask if the group members have ever asked God for help to change. Discuss what reasons people might have for not asking for this help. "

Thought:
With God's help, Peter was able to change

Total Time: up to 30 minutes

Make over  10 minutes

Make a large outline figure of a man to represent the disciple Peter. Prepare a set of cards each with one of the following Bible references on side A: Matthew 16:21–23; Mark 14:49–51; Luke 22:54–62; John 18:10; John 13:36–38. Write one of the following references on side B of each card: Acts 2:14, 40–41; Acts 4:13,14, 18–21; Acts 4:7–10.

Divide into pairs giving each pair one of the cards (duplicate cards as necessary) and ask the group members to decide on one word which describes Peter's behaviour/character in the Bible incident on side A of their card. Brainstorm these answers and write them on the outline figure. The answers may well include headstrong, hasty, bigheaded, cowardly, disloyal etc.

Commentator 10 minutes

" You may want to expand on any of the characteristics or incidents, and then express surprise that Peter was actually one of Jesus' best friends. Why would Jesus choose such a person to be his disciple?

Now ask the pairs to turn over their card and read the incident on side B. Ask them to sum up Peter's behaviour/character in one word and brainstorm the answers. As suggestions are called out, write them up alongside the contrasting characteristics already on the figure and cross through the old characteristics. For example, disloyal may be changed to loyal, cowardly to bold.

Chequered Flag 7 minutes

We might not bite our nails but we all suffer from some of the bad habits described in the Bible. However, we have a God who wants to come alongside us and work with us, changing us for the better, enabling us to display the qualities which he originally intended us to possess.

Write the following on a board or enlarge and copy it:

towenknowenthatotinytallinthingsogGodoework styforeotherigoodyewithemthosew owhomeloventhimum.

See who can crack the code first.
(Answer: Romans 8:28)

On the Podium 2 minutes

Award prizes for the following activities: *Nail-biting*, *The bleep machine*, *I can't stop!*, *Play your cards right*, *Good habits* and *Gearing for a problem*.

Lap of Honour 10 minutes

Get it polished!
Give individuals or pairs items which are dirty in someway, eg brass ornaments that need polishing. Give them the equipment they need to clean or polish them and ask them to try and make a difference to the item you have given them. Play a song in the background, such as 'Jesus you are changing me' by Marilyn Baker (found in 1990 edition of The Spring Harvest Song Book).

Finish by having a look at each individual's or pair's work, and close with a prayer of thanksgiving for Jesus' willingness to help change us into better people.

Forgiveness

Qualifying

Group members will know what it's like to be hurt by others in some way which, if not resolved, can result in further conflict. This session seeks to encourage the group members to think seriously about forgiveness by highlighting the example and teachings of Jesus.

Although this session touches on the forgiveness Christ bought for us all on the cross, it doesn't go into great detail. Members of your group may not understand why Jesus had to die and rise again. Be prepared to explain this fundamental part of the gospel in a full but understandable way.

It may be useful to have some simple tracts to help you out, such as the HEY tract produced by CPO (tel 01903 264556).

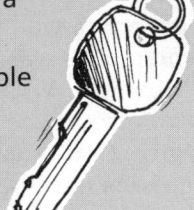

Starting Grid
(up to 20 minutes)

As forgiveness has to do with changing how you feel about someone and forgetting their hurtful behaviour, here are a few activities which will help introduce these ideas.

A Peaceful and wayward — 10 minutes

This is an adaptation of the popular game, Port and Starboard. The leader calls out the following instructions in any order and the group members do the actions associated with them. The last member to do the action in each case is out. Play until you have some winners.

Argue: players point fingers at leader
Fight: players put fists in the air
Hurt: players collapse on the floor
Scarper left: players run to the left of the hall
Scarper right: players run to the right of the hall
Sorry: players fall on their knees in a begging position
Forgive: players find one other partner and shake hands with them
Forget: players scratch their heads
Friends: players find another partner and give them a piggy back

B Forget the answers — 10 minutes

Before this game, make up 10–15 general knowledge questions, print them (and the answers) on paper ready for distribution amongst the group. Explain that you are going to give them a little test, but that you are going to be generous and give them the questions and answers to look over beforehand. Hand out the previously prepared sheets and allow them to look at them for about two minutes. Collect them all in and then hand out pieces of paper. Ask the first question and then explain that the winner is the person who can answer the most questions incorrectly! Go through the answers and award points/prizes.

Commentator
 1 minute

" Today we are looking at the topic of forgiveness, the process whereby you choose to stop yourself feeling angry and resentful towards another person and choose to forget their hurtful behaviour. "

Thought:
How forgiving am I?

Total Time: 16 minutes

Confessions — 15 minutes

Before the session, have prepared newspaper cuttings which describe both petty and serious crimes. Create some relevant scenarios from which group members will have to decide if they will forgive the offenders or not. Label two opposite walls of your meeting room 'Forgiven' and 'Not forgiven'.

Give each group member a piece of paper and a pen and ask them to (anonymously) write down something that they may have done wrong in the past, which can then be read out. It may have been participating in a practical joke which went wrong, bullying, stealing, lying etc. Ask them to place their misdemeanours in a box at the front.

Read at random either a newspaper cutting, a scenario or one of the group's misdemeanours. The group members are to place themselves in the victim's shoes and make an individual decision as to whether or not they personally would forgive the offender. If they would definitely forgive or not forgive the person, then they are to stand by the appropriate wall. If they are not sure, they are to stand a little way from the wall nearest to their inclination. When they have made their decision, pick on someone to ask why they would/would not forgive. Continue this activity until many relevant scenarios have been raised.

Find out in what situations group members are/are not prepared to forgive.

Commentator

1 minute

"Throughout our lives we will all face situations where we will hurt others and they will hurt us. When we are hurt by someone's behaviour or words, we have a choice to make. Do we hold onto the hurt and resentment, thus subsequently mistreating the offender? Or do we choose to forgive the offending party and forget about the misdemeanours? This is a difficult decision to make, as revenge, not forgiveness, is often seen as the best option. How did Jesus react when placed in such situations?"

Thought:
Jesus led by example, forgiving even when it was hard.

Total Time: 18 minutes

Forgiven or not?

15 minutes

Split the group into two teams. Place the two sets of cards from the activity on page 18 ('Jesus' suffering') on a board in front of the teams – one set for team A, the other for team B. These are all the things that Jesus suffered on his way to the cross.

Explain that you will read some verses from the Bible, changing some of the details from the biblical account. The first person who recognises where a mistake has been made and puts a hand up explaining where the mistake was, wins control of the game for the team. One of the cards is then removed from their set, showing that the suffering has been forgiven. If that same team can say what the correct answer should be, they have another card taken from their set. If they answer incorrectly, the other team can have a chance of answering and having a card taken from their set.

Read through John 8:1–11 changing some words eg, 'Jesus went to the Mount of Pizzas (olives). At dawn he appeared again in the bus queue (temple courts), where all the turnips (people) gathered square him (around him).'

Wherever you are in the passage, when you see a hand raised stop reading and go through the above instructions. Each time you stop, reread the passage from the previous sentence or from the beginning so that the group members can grasp the true story. Remember to read quite slowly!

The winning team is the one with the least cards left on the board, signifying that they are the 'most' forgiven.

If a team loses all its cards before the completion of the passage, congratulate the team for winning, but continue playing the game to see if the other team can end up in the same state.

NB Do not read the proper passage to them first. Let them try and guess the correct answers.

Commentator

3 minutes

"In the passage we have just read, Jesus was confronted with a dilemma: should he or shouldn't he forgive the woman who had broken the Jewish law? This was a very important question for Jesus and the woman involved as it was, for her, a life and death situation. After Jesus pointed out the fact that we all do wrong, her accusers left her. This left only Jesus. Would he forgive her or not? He did, but told her to stop doing the wrong things she was involved in.

In another situation we read of all the awful things that people did towards Jesus, treatment which would surely leave someone feeling bitter, resentful and angry towards the perpetrators. Yet despite his pain and suffering, when Jesus was on the cross, he cried out: 'Father, forgive them, for they do not know what they are doing' (Luke 23:34). Amazingly when Jesus was pushed to the limit and he was facing death, he still chose to forgive.

This may be OK for Jesus, but does that mean I have to forgive others too?"

Thought:
Why should I forgive?

Total Time: 10 minutes

Barrier
5 minutes

Split the group into pairs.
Give each pair an enlarged copy of the game board on the activity sheet (see page 88), plus a dice. Label one person A and the other B and play as per instructions on the sheet. After five minutes note their individual scores.

Commentator
5 minutes

" Jesus forgave people but what about us? Do we have to? Not forgiving is like a barrier which builds up between people just like the barrier in the game: as it grew it became harder to get round. Ultimately unforgiveness will spoil us by potentially making us bitter and angry. This hurts other people as well as ourselves, but most importantly will prevent us knowing God and his forgiveness. "

Chequered Flag *12 minutes*

Explain that forgiveness is often not seen as a credible option but, as God demonstrated through Jesus time and again, forgiving is God's way of handling hurtful situations. By forgiving others, we can have a strong relationship with God and with others, and not be spoilt by bitterness and resentment.

Read 'The parable of the unforgiving servant' from Matthew 18:21–35. Explain that ultimately the decision to forgive is ours. How will the knowledge of our forgiving God affect our behaviour?

On the Podium *5 minutes*

Award the prizes for the following activities: *Peaceful and wayward*, *Forget the answers* and *Forgiven or not?*.

Lap of Honour *8 minutes*

Spend some time focussing on God and the fact that he's forgiven us through Jesus' death and resurrection. One way to do this is as follows:

Breaking walls

Ask the group to make a tall wall with cardboard boxes. Once erected, label the wall 'sin' and explain that when we choose to please ourselves rather than God, we are separated from him. However, because of the forgiveness Jesus won for us on the cross, those who choose to believe in him can have a relationship with him. Ask the group to write a 'thank you' to God on a piece of paper and tape it to one of their shoes. Stand in a line and at your signal, throw the shoes at the wall to break it down, demonstrating that a new start with God can be possible.

Barrier

			Wrongs you have done			
			not forgive the			
			your Father will			
			forgive others, then			
			you do not			
			you. But if			
			will also forgive			
			Father in heaven			
			to you, your			
			they have done			
			others the wrongs			
Square A			If you forgive			Square B

Person A starts from square A and person B starts from square B. The idea is to see how many times you can cross from either square A to B or vice versa in the given time. You move by throwing the dice. Each time you complete a crossing, you score 1 point.

If you roll a 1 or 4, colour in the lowest available Bible verse square on the sheet. This then becomes a barrier and so when you move, you have to move around it (without moving diagonally), thus making your journey to square A or B longer.

Prejudice

Qualifying

Our society is full of people of all ages who feel they have been discriminated against in some way. This session explores what prejudice is and the forms it takes. It points out that when people were prejudiced against Jesus, he prayed to his Father and sought to educate his listeners, focusing on the way God wanted people to be treated: as equally important, valuable people.

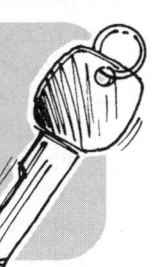

Starting Grid

(up to 20 minutes)

A Stereotypes — 6 minutes

Split the group into teams of four.
Two from each team go to one end of the room, the other two go to the opposite end. Give each pair some paper and a pencil. Call out descriptions of different people (eg a mad professor, a vicar, a train spotter, a life guard, a bungee jumper etc) and ask them to draw what they think the named person would look like, along with any associated props.

Both pairs are to do this without showing the other their ideas. Compare the two pictures drawn by each team, and award one point each for the similarities expressed in their drawings.

B Acquiring the facts — 10 minutes

REW ◀◀ Using the same teams as above, choose one volunteer from each to sit at the front of the room, facing the rest of the group. Explain that each volunteer represents their team and has the opportunity of scoring points for the team.

This challenge is all about courage and overcoming fears they may have regarding certain foods. Reveal foods such as lychees, lime pickle, yoghurt, tripe, avocado or other less common foods. Discover whether or not each volunteer will take a taste of each of them. If they do, they receive 20 points for each food tasted.

Note the reactions of the volunteers as they will help you make the point that we often make judgements about someone or something without knowing the full facts.

C The biased referee — 10 minutes

Play some general team games.
Gradually become biased towards one team and see how long it takes for anyone to notice.

Commentator

⏱ 2 minutes

"We can all have stereotypes, a fixed idea about what someone or something is like. We need to keep a check on such opinions as they can lead us to show an unreasonable dislike for someone or something because of what we think they're like. Often this arises because someone forms an opinion without knowing all the facts. Have you ever had such an experience?"

Thought:
Experiences of prejudice

Total Time: 25 minutes

The prejudice experience — 20 minutes

REW ◀◀ Photocopy the game board on page 92 and prepare the following list for display: 1 Racism, 2 Sexism, 3 Ageism, 4 Rich/Poor, 5 Disability, 6 Religion.

Split the group into four teams and give each team a colour. Put their coloured counters in the numbered positions on the board. Each team takes it in turns to throw a dice, trying to throw a 1 or 6 to start. First move one of their counters to the shaded start square on the outside of the board. They then throw again and move in a clockwise direction around the board.

Once a counter has been moved completely around the board and they reach their entry square again, the counter can be placed in one of the shaded squares in the centre of the board.

Once a team has more than one counter on the board, they can split their dice score between them.

The team with the most pieces in the centre of the board at the end of the allotted time, wins.

If a team lands on an opposing team's counter, they

have the opportunity to send that team's counter back to its base to start its journey again. This is done in the following way:

If a red lands on a blue, for example, the blue team roll the dice to choose a type of prejudice from the prepared list for the red team to think about eg, if 1 is thrown then the subject chosen for the red team is racism. The red team then throws the dice to determine the degree of prejudice encountered and have to come up with an appropriate example. (1= a mild example of racial prejudice ie, choosing not to sit next to someone on a bus because of the colour of their skin, and 6 = an extreme example of prejudice ie, killing someone because of their colour of their skin.) If the red team's example is judged to be satisfactory, then remove the counter of the blue team.

Commentator

5 minutes

"As we all have experienced prejudice ourselves or seen people suffer as a result of some form of prejudice, ask the group how people react when they become victims. See if they can come up with any guidelines a) for coping with prejudice and b) if they realise they are prejudiced towards others.

Congratulate them on their answers and explain that you are going to look at how Jesus coped when he suffered from prejudice."

Thought:
Coping with prejudice

Total Time: 10 minutes

Card quiz

6 minutes

Read Mark 6:1–5 to the group.
Write out the following on separate cards, making a set for each team. Shuffle them and see who can be the first to correctly make the questions raised in the passage.

Where did / he get / all this?
What wisdom / is this / that has / been given him?
How does / he perform miracles?
Isn't he the / carpenter, the son / of Mary, and / the brother of / James, Joseph, Judas / and Simon?
Aren't his / sisters living / here?

Commentator

4 minutes

"Those in Jesus' home town couldn't understand why Jesus taught in the powerful way that he did – after all, wasn't he just the carpenter, a simpleton, the son of Mary and no one of any great significance?

The people in Jesus' home town had a picture of him in their minds which he was supposed to conform to. Their prejudice towards him was revealed through their actions when they dismissed him, rejected him and became violent towards him (Luke 4:29).

How did Jesus handle such prejudice? We are told that he regularly prayed to his Father (Mark 1:35–39; Luke 4:42–44), but he also practically set about educating others."

Thought:
What can we learn from the Good Samaritan? (Luke 10:25-37)

Total Time: 30 minutes

Choose one of the following activities to explore this passage further.

Ⓐ The silent movie

25 minutes

Split the group into four teams: one to provide the sound, one to provide the writing boards and two to act out the story. Read the passage to them. Explain that you would like to make a silent movie of the incident and that each team will be responsible for a different part of the 'film'.

Give each team a list of these headings:
A 'Who is my neighbour?' (title)
B Man attacked on road
C Priest ignores man
D Levite ignores man
E Samaritan carries out first aid
F Samaritan takes man to inn
G Samaritan pays for man's upkeep

Provide the sound group with musical instruments and ask them to create different sounds for the different sections of the story. Provide the group making the boards with large sheets of card or paper for them to write the introduction of each section on. They should also write any sentences that the drama groups wish to emphasise. The drama groups divide the sections equally so that each team looks at different sections and devises a short silent sketch for each.

Perform the drama and, if possible, film it.

A Spontaneous drama — 10 minutes

Split the group into teams.
Read the passage slowly, emphasising the key verbs. Ask the teams to act it out as you go along. Video the final performance and show it.

Commentator — 5 minutes

"Jesus told this story as a response to the question 'Who is my neighbour?' (Luke 10:29), which arose after he spoke about one of the key commandments: 'Love your neighbour as you love yourself' (Luke 10:27).

Jesus used a Samaritan as the hero of the passage because Jews hated Samaritans. Through the passage Jesus teaches that caring for those in need is a fulfilment of the commandment because everyone is special, important and loved by God. The following Bible passage reinforces the point: there is no excuse for prejudice in God's eyes. Read Acts 10:34,35."

Chequered Flag — 3 minutes

Prejudice can occur when someone decides to take a discriminatory course of action based upon a fixed set of ideas which are incorrect. Unfortunately many people are the victims of prejudice, but as we have seen, so was Jesus.

Jesus tackled the situation by praying to his Father and setting about educating his listeners in the way God views people – that is, equally – and so encouraged people to follow his example. We can learn from the way Jesus approached prejudice either when we are victims ourselves or when we know others who are. Read Philippians 4:12,13 and point out that we can take encouragement from the truth which Paul, an apostle of Jesus, discovered when he went through hard times.

On the Podium — 5 minutes

Award prizes for the following activities: *Stereotypes*, *Acquiring the facts*, *The biased referee*, *The prejudice experience* and *The card quiz*.

Lap of Honour — 8 minutes

Item pick

God doesn't judge by outward appearances (Galatians 2:6), but looks at the heart (1 Samuel 16:7). How do we look to God?

Show the group some items on a tray, for example a picture; toy figure such as a soldier; notepad; mirror. Ask them to choose one which they feel represents their heart ie the place of their innermost thoughts. Don't ask them to explain why they chose what they did, simply close by thanking God for all the positive things that he sees in each of us and pray that he'll deal with the things which don't look good to him.

The Prejudice EXPERIENCE

ACTIVITY SHEET 19

				Start	→			
		1 pink	2 pink	3 pink	4 pink	5 pink		
	1 blue			6 pink			1 grey	
↑	2 blue						2 grey	
Start	3 blue	6 blue				6 grey	3 grey	Start
	4 blue						4 grey	↓
	5 blue			6 red			5 grey	
		1 red	2 red	3 red	4 red	5 red		
			←	Start				

Jesus for me?

Qualifying

This session aims to challenge all the young people have learnt about Jesus and encourages them to make a response. Ensure that you have suitable literature available and that you have at least one follow-up session after this, before having a break in your programme.

The session has a different format from the rest of the book, as it only has two laps. Make this last session into a celebratory meal/party night, so that the Parable of the Great Banquet may be understood in the light of it. However, if this is not possible, there should be enough material in the remaining activities to make this session special.

Starting Grid
(up to 20 minutes)

The following activities remind the group just how special Jesus is.

Ⓐ The attractions quiz  up to 20 minutes

REW ◀◀ Consult various magazines so that you build up a list of questions on the following subjects:

1) TV soaps
2) Adverts
3) Pictures and posters
4) Christianity
5) Music
6) Films

Split the group into teams. Each team throws a dice – the number rolled dictates from which category a question is asked (see above). The first person to put up their hand and answer correctly wins a point for their team. Play for as long as you like.

Ⓑ Jesus' qualities  8 minutes

REW ◀◀ Split the group into teams with a piece of paper and pen. Ask the teams to try and come up with one of the qualities of Jesus for each letter of the alphabet.

Ⓒ Blockbusters  upto 20 minutes

REW ◀◀ If you didn't use the Blockbusters game on page 66, this would be a good place to use it.

Ⓓ Jesus' claims  up to 15 minutes

REW ◀◀ Make up two identical sets of cards with one of the following claims of Jesus written on each:

The Messiah (John 4:26);
The Bread of Life (John 6:35);
The One from Above (John 8:23);
The Eternal One (John 8:58);
The Light Of The World (John 4:5);
The Gate (John 10:7);
The Son of God (John 10:36);
The Resurrection and The Life (John 11:25);
The Lord and Master (John 13:13);
The Way, Truth and the Life (John 14:6);
The True Vine (John 15:1);
The Alpha and Omega (Rev 1:8);
The First and Last (Rev 1:17).

Spread out the cards face down. Take turns turning over the cards two at a time until all the pairs have been matched up.

Thought:
Jesus' words can be relied on

Total Time: 20 minutes

Puzzle it out  7 minutes

Write the following on paper and give a copy to each team:

When ___ ___ saying ___ ___, the ___ was ___ at ___ ___ he ___.

He ___ like the ___ of the ___; instead, ___ ___ with ___.

(Matthew 7:28,29, GNB).

Give each team the missing words written on cards, plus seven extra ones as red herrings. Discover which team can complete the verse the quickest.

Commentator
2 minutes

"When Jesus began teaching people about God and his ways, his listeners soon realised that his teaching was very special, and different to that of the other religious leaders of the day. This was because Jesus talked about God from firsthand experience and others could only use what was found in the Jewish scriptures.

How did Jesus know God from firsthand experience?"

Activity sheet
10 minutes

Photocopy enough activity sheets (see page 96) for one per team, and cut each into pieces along the grid lines. Give one member of each team the set of pieces and a dice. This member then goes and sits with one of the other teams.

On your command each team throws a dice. They are given a square of the worksheet which corresponds to the number of their dice roll. See which team can obtain all the pieces of the activity sheet and assemble them first.

Commentator
2 minutes

"Jesus knew the ways of God because he is God, a fact which we may never fully understand. What this tells us about God is that he came to show and prepare the way for us to have a relationship with him, in person, because he values and loves us so much. No wonder people marvelled and were amazed by Jesus and his teaching! We can totally trust Jesus' words. Do we?"

Thought:
As Jesus can be trusted let us take heed of 'The parable of the great banquet' (Luke 14:15–24).

Total Time: An hour plus

The banquet
60 minutes

Option 1
As this is the last session, make the occasion really special by having a banquet. You could have a buffet, party games and a disco. Alternatively, why not ask members to come to the session in their best clothes, turn your meeting room into a five-star restaurant with all the trimmings (eg candles, napkins, name placings) and provide a full sit-down meal for them. You could have burger and chips, or go the full way and have a roast dinner! The young people will love being waited upon by the leaders.

Commentator
5 minutes

"After everyone has had their meal, ask the group whether they have enjoyed themselves, and what they may have felt like if they had missed out on the meal/activities. Retell the parable in your own words to the group and apply it. (Refer to the following commentator section.)"

Option 2 (25 minutes)
If the above activity is not possible, then retell the parable to your group in your own words. As a group, make a large painted mural, which describes how the scene may have looked. As it starts to dry, do the following activity:

The excuse game
10 minutes

On cards, write down different situations in which people make excuses eg, handing in late homework, failing an exam, speeding. Split the group into teams. In turn each team chooses a card and is given 30 seconds to come up with as many excuses as possible for the given situation. Award the team a point for each acceptable excuse. The team with the most points wins.

Commentator
5 minutes

"Jesus told this parable to try and show that we all are invited into God's kingdom; a kingdom which overflows with many wonderful things, which can be ours now, not just when we die. Through Jesus, God invites us all into his family to taste the many different things he reserves for his sons and daughters. However, despite God's wonderful gifts, many people miss out because they make excuses and refuse to believe that God's kingdom is as good as he says it is. They choose instead to do their own thing.

Jesus invites us all to become part of his Father's family. To illustrate this, make up an invitation card for each person using the following text:

'Dear... I Jesus invite you to come into my father's family to become his child, and my friend. We love and value you so much that your entrance fee has already been paid, through my death. It cost me everything, but it was worth it, just for you. I look forward to your response, Jesus.'

You must decide how far you want to challenge the young people and how you want to see them respond, but please ensure that:

a) any young person who does respond, realises that being a Christian is not an easy way through life, but can be the harder choice to make;

b) those who respond are fed into discipleship groups. "

Chequered Flag 2 minutes

Jesus showed that he was someone extremely special through all the things he said and did. People soon noticed that he didn't speak from secondhand experience, but he really knew God. He had come to make a way for us to have a relationship with God.

Such a relationship qualifies us as God's children and allows us to tap into all the wonderful things that are in his kingdom. This doesn't exclude us from experiencing hassles in life, but does give us the resources to cope with them when they arise.

Some choose to excuse themselves from receiving such a wonderful inheritance from God and instead choose to go it alone. Whatever their reasons may be, we are left in no doubt that such people will miss out on the best that God has to offer. How are we to respond to God's invitation?

On the Podium 5 minutes

Award prizes for the following activities: *The attractions quiz*, *Jesus' qualities*, *Jesus' claims*, *The activity sheet* and *The excuse game*.

Lap of Honour 5 minutes

A toast to Jesus

Give everyone a drink and, in banqueting tradition, ask people to propose a toast to Jesus, using the things that they want to thank him for.

The Father and I are one
John 10 : 30

1	2	3
4	5	6
1	2	3
4	5	6
1	2	3
4	5	6

Son Holy Spirit Father